GUN GUIDE FOR DEMOCRATS

GUN GUIDE FOR DEMOCRATS

How to Avoid a Second American Civil War

Christopher Hurst

© 2022 By Kilimanjaro Kutembea Publishing, Wind River Associates, Inc.

All rights reserved. No part of this publication may be reproduced, distributed, or transmitted in any form or by any means, including photocopying, recording, or other electronic or mechanical methods, without the prior written permission of the publisher, except in the case of brief quotations embodied in critical reviews and specific other noncommercial uses permitted by copyright law.

For permission requests, commercial orders, or media inquiries, please contact us at:

Kilimanjaro Kutembea Publishing
Wind River Associates, Inc.
62504 Indian Summer Way E
Enumclaw, WA 98022

Print Book ISBN: 9798396169593

eBook ISBN: Not currently offered as an eBook

Printed in the United States of America & Overseas by Kindle Direct Publishing
First Edition, May 5, 2022 (Original)
Second Version May 9, 2023
(Originally Titled - Shooting Liberally – A Gun Guide for Democrats & Independents in a Time of Political Division)

Note that the information in this book contains topics and techniques that can be dangerous. Always follow all rules from the manufacturers of all weapons and accessories or ammunition fully, as well as all local, state, and federal laws at all times. This book is academic in nature rather than an instructional study of social, political, and self-defense topics and should never replace individual professional instruction and training. The author, publisher, and distributor disclaim all liability from loss, injury, or damage, personal or otherwise, resulting from the information and procedures in this book.

INDEX OF CHAPTERS

PART ONE – The Fun & Interesting Stuff

Introduction	3
Chapter One – Fascism in America	9
Chapter Two - The Nazi Swine	17
Chapter Three – The Second Amendment Isn't Just for Rednecks	23
Chapter Four - Who is Buying Guns Now, and Why?	27
Chapter Five - A Brief History of Firearms	33
Chapter Six – How Accurate Are Guns?	41
Chapter Seven – Killing People	47
Chapter Eight - Advanced Training	63
Chapter Nine – Self-Assessment - Take a Seat on the Couch	67
Chapter Ten – Negligence & The Very End of Your Life	75
Chapter Eleven– How a Bullet Kills	77

Chapter Twelve – Home Defense Alternatives	87
Chapter Thirteen – Home Invasion Robberies	97
Chapter Fourteen – Basic Types of Firearms for Sale Today	101
Chapter Fifteen – Choosing Your Firearm	107
Chapter Sixteen – What to Hide and Where to Hide It	127
Chapter Seventeen – Fight Club for Democrats	135
Chapter Eighteen - Snitches Get Stitches	139
Chapter Nineteen – O Canada! & War in Europe	147
Chapter Twenty - A Thousand Easy Pieces	153

PART TWO - The Less Interesting Stuff That Could Save Your Life

Chapter Twenty-one – Firearm Safety in Your Home	159
Chapter Twenty-two – Personal Firearm Safety	173
Chapter Twenty-three – Range Safety	183
Chapter Twenty-four – Firing Wild – Guns in the Forest	187
Chapter Twenty-five – A Visual Basic Summary of Firearms & Terms	193
Chapter Twenty-six – Bullet Details	207
Closing Notes	213

PART ONE

THE FUN & INTERESTING STUFF

President Trump's insurrection on the steps of the U.S. Capitol, January 6, 2021. Credit Michael Brochstein, ZUMA Wire, Alamy Live News.

INTRODUCTION

I am a Democrat. I served as an elected Washington State House of Representatives member for 14 years. I am also an expert in using and handling all types of firearms. That is because I am also a retired 25-year veteran police detective. I ended my law enforcement career as the Commander of a 15-city Homicide & Violent Crimes Task Force. I served over 1,400 search warrants for most crimes, including child rape, kidnapping, violent assault, drugs, and murder. There are few tactical or shooting situations I have not seen first-hand.

Most of my friends are liberal, but I also try to get along with my more conservative friends, at least the ones who still talk to me. Many have broken off those relationships, even within families. I try to talk to everyone.

Many liberal or Democratic friends recently came to me for odd advice. Some want to know more about firearms in general. They assume I know a lot about them, and I do. Some are more specific and ask what type of gun they should get. Some are worried about other Americans having guns. They want to understand and assess the risk of their fellow citizens being armed, especially after seeing the events on January 6, 2021.

Others are concerned that the U.S. is at risk of a second Civil War. They believe a gun might become necessary if a Trumpian or DeSantis-style dictatorship were to take over America. Former President Donald Trump and his supporters not only attempted to overturn our election in 2020 but are now working to restrict future free and fair elections. They support Trump's false claim that he did not overwhelmingly lose that election.

Despite many repeated false allegations, extensive investigations, and legal challenges, no voter fraud that would have changed the election's outcome was detected. Trump lost the election by over seven million votes. When I say "Trumpian" or "Trumpists" in this book, I am not referring to all voters who have supported Donald Trump at the polls. I am using those terms as a shorthand way of referring to people who insist that the 2020 election was stolen, no matter who they currently support as the leader of their radical political cult.

Facts are not stopping these people from arming themselves in preparation for taking over America. Their plans rely upon their opponents, liberals, and Democrats, not being armed and opposing them, not unlike what happened to the people of Germany in the 1930s. That mistake led to millions of Germans and over 60 million people being killed worldwide because of the nationalist regimes in Germany, Japan, and Italy. Many German citizens opposed to Hitler or deemed "undesirables" were exterminated in gas chambers and death camps. Six million Jews from Europe were executed in the Holocaust simply because they were Jewish. Comparisons of then and now might sound extreme – but consider how seemingly low-key it all started.

Some of this interest in guns by liberals and Democrats surprised me, but I see a clear trend in why people feel unsafe. There are three main reasons: First, people on the right already have guns, especially military assault-style weapons. Liberals and Democrats feel they may need to defend themselves with guns. Second, over half of Americans believe that a second Civil War is entirely possible. This is a chilling thought. People wish to acquire firearms if we lose our democracy and enter a dictatorship without our legislative and judicial branches of government to protect us. Third, if a dictatorial regime rises, people want to support a resistance organization. They want to fight or supply weapons for those fighting to restore our freedom.

The founders of America were concerned that a dictatorship, not unlike a repressive King or a church/state government, might someday arise here. They fled England to get away from one. The Second Amendment to the United States Constitution is all about that.

Asking about getting a gun, or what type to get, indicates a decision level of significance for liberal folks. It is a turning point.

Most Americans, even those with guns, know too little about them and even less about shooting encounters. This book will provide information about the state of gun ownership in America.

It will explain using a firearm properly and safely. A person who reads, understands, and accepts the lessons in this book will be far more informed than most American gun owners.

The initial question, "Should I own a gun?" is complex. The answer may be vastly different from what you expected. Before owning a firearm, one must know the basics about firearms, safety, and killing another person.

Many of my conservative-leaning friends have met the concept of this book with the shock that liberals, Democrats, and communities of color might think of getting guns. They've always assumed that guns were entirely their domain. But the coming years will see liberals, Democrats, and communities of color making up most of the market for new gun sales in America.

Much of this book will be new to people who don't have guns. Some parts will be surprising. Some of it will, out of necessity, be shocking. I have seen plenty of people injured and dead from firearms. Guns, gunfights, and firearm injuries are nothing like you will ever see on TV, in a movie, or in a video game. Although I will omit the ghastliest details, some information will be necessary for you to fully understand the responsibilities of gun ownership and the effects of using a gun to kill someone.

We are the only gun-owning country in the world with such a deficit of expertise among gun owners. Some countries have high percentages of gun ownership, but only a fraction of the gun violence, accidents, murders, and shootings happening in America. Gun ownership does not need to make a society unsafe, but gun ignorance does.

This book is not intended to be overtly political, except when America faces fascism and new-era Nazis in our country. WWII and Hitler taught us that you could not negotiate with fascists or Nazis. They see attempts to have a dialog as a weakness to be exploited. They have no regard for any concept of public policy or collective well-being. They will never agree to share power with any other person or institution. These principles have not changed since the rise of Hitler, Mussolini, and Tojo in Germany, Italy, and Japan before WWII. No civilized society should give them safe harbor. They will find none in this book.

Regarding other political views, I will make statements that some liberals will find offensive – for example, like it or not, Second Amendment rights are currently settled law in America. Further, adequately regulated firearm ownership is not necessarily dangerous in a free country. On the other hand, I will offend some conservatives who refuse to accept that Trumpists attempted an insurrection to reverse the presidential election on January 6, 2021, and that we came perilously close to losing our democratic republic on that day.

Much of this book is about people considering arming themselves and preparing a defense should others decide not to respect the majority rule and the lives and liberty of all citizens. January 6th taught us that we have enough national instability already. There is a current risk of unrest that can lead to more violence unless things change. As Americans, we are all in this together. In my opinion, we should treat our right-of-center friends and fellow countrymen with respect and calm deliberation, work hard for reconciliation, but plan for the risk of a storm on the horizon we can all foresee.

Liberals, Democrats, and people of color safely arming themselves can provide a significant deterrent to the plans of some radical Trumpists to end our democratic republic. Trumpists will be much more reluctant to attempt a takeover if they face opposition. We can keep our democracy from failing. Our founding fathers had this in mind when our country was formed. This is what the Second Amendment and our right to bear arms are for - our defense against tyranny.

August 12, 2017. White supremacists gather for the Unite the Right rally in Charlottesville, Virginia, Sean Rayford, Alamy Photo

CHAPTER ONE

FASCISM IN AMERICA

It is essential to identify the players in the current American political system. No longer just Democrats, Independents, and Republicans, extremism has given rise to something new in our country. Extreme radical fundamentalists who have blended religion and politics have exploded under the watch of Trump. Beliefs have replaced reason. Blind loyalty to a man has replaced a social obligation to our country and fellow Americans. Trump and his followers have suggested removing the courts and the Constitution itself. They have taken up arms in staggering numbers to see this done. They openly call for a second American Civil War to install Trump as our dictator and religious ruler. This is by no means everyone who voted for Trump, and there is pushback against this movement by some mainstream Republicans, but its membership numbers in the millions of people today. You have undoubtedly met and talked to some of them, and some may be in your family. In the first few years of this Trump movement, no one wanted to think we had fascists or Nazis in our midst, and journalists were reluctant to call them such. But today, it is clear who and what they are. So, let's explore that definition and then consider what that means in this discussion about firearms and your safety.

People often use the terms "fascism" and "Nazis," but some do not even know what they mean. Fascism is a far-right ultra-nationalism dictatorship, suppression of opposition, and regimentation of society, and it is dangerous. Nazism was the dogma of the Nationalist Socialist German Workers Party under Hitler during the 1930s and 1940s, and today means extremely racist and authoritarian behavior. Some people use these terms anytime a law passes or executive orders are issued that they do not like. They call it fascism.

On the contrary, even though you hear it frequently, Americans are still free to vote for their government, their votes are counted, and all three branches of our government are functioning. People can contest any law or order they do not like in the courts. Any contested law or order found to violate the Constitution is nullified. There is no fascist government today in America. No one person can declare any law or order unconstitutional themselves or just by saying that it is. That is anarchy. We govern ourselves collectively, and that is democracy. It does a great disservice, demeaning the work of the men and women who have fought for our nation against real fascists and Nazis, to complain that any law one dislikes is "fascism."

Fascism takes power away from the other branches of government and consolidates it in the dictatorship. Fascism's first step is to overturn free and fair elections and eventually to end voting altogether, something Trump-style election deniers are trying to do today in many states and got close to accomplishing during their insurrection on January 6, 2021.

Since the coup attempt on the United States Capitol on January 6, 2021, America's confidence in the strength of our country has been shaken. By the end of 2021, a plurality of all Americans believed we were headed toward a second Civil War. Over 60% of Americans are at least apprehensive about it. But many partisan supporters of Trumpism welcome a second Civil War and see it as a good, if not a necessary development, to help bring a Trumpian-style dictatorship to America.

Folks buying weapons and ammunition to help usher in a fascist Trumpian dictatorship have been stockpiling weapons and bullets for years. The Southern Poverty Law Center, an institution that works for civil rights and tracks hate groups, documents these groups and their dramatic increase in the era of Trump and deems them dangerous.

We have members of the insurrectionist organizations Proud Boys and Oath Keepers in my part of the country. One local group predominately anti-Jewish and anti-Black is the "Atomwaffen Division." I have often seen them in the forests in their signature uniforms and quasi-tactical gear. They wear pro-Hitler messages and Swastikas. These self-described Nazi idealists often wear masks to hide their identities, but then some post undisguised pictures and videos of themselves on the internet! They can't help it.

Usually, they blast away and don't seem to understand anything about real tactical training with their weapons. People with police or military training would laugh at their "training" sessions in the woods.

Several members of the "Atomwaffen Division" are now in Federal prison or awaiting their trials and sentences for their overtly terrorist activities. They have been involved in weapons violations, drug dealing, and transportation and power systems threats. They have also publicly posted anti-Semitic posters and threatened journalists in the Seattle area who were reporting on them. One local reporter specifically threatened after investigating them was Chris Ingalls of KING-5 News. He has given interviews that you can find online about how these threats affected him. Their downfall? An FBI informant. I will explain more about that later in a Chapter called "Snitches Get Stitches."

The leader of the Oath Keepers, Elmer Stewart Rhodes, has been charged with seditious conspiracy. Henry "Enrique" Tarrio of the Proud Boys was indicted for their organization's actions on January 6th, 2021. After the first version of this book was published, the leaders of the Proud Boys and Oath Keepers were convicted in court and are facing decades in prison. At the trial, the United States Attorney called them "Trump's Army." They were just that, like Hitler's Brown Shirts in the 1930s.

Although dangerous, the groups named by the Southern Poverty Law Center are not necessarily the worst ones we should be most afraid of. The ones we don't hear about pose a greater risk. People are arming themselves who adhere to Trumpism and keep to themselves. They are cautious of others finding out about their activities and plans. Often, they are heavily armed and, in some cases, better trained in using and handling more complex military weapons. They are not a majority of the run-of-the-mill far-right gun owners, but they are a sizable group. I have come across many of them in the forests. They tend to know what they are doing with military-style weapons and have at least a rudimentary level of tactical training. A sign of them is often a large swastika tattooed on their neck or information on them or their vehicles indicating adherence to the QAnon beliefs, usually in a code not meant to be understood by outsiders. Sometimes more overt statements of these beliefs come from people like Republican Congresswoman Marjorie Taylor-Green from Georgia, who also said that blue Jewish lasers had started California forest fires from outer space, but many others are more secretive.

There is a misperception that the disloyal insurrectionists of January 6, 2021, were predominately former military combat veterans. That is not true. The insurrectionists were primarily people who dressed up and posed as combat veterans. Loyal American combat veterans do not support such activities. Many people pretend to be combat veterans when they are not.

The real problem for our society is that no matter whether they are trained or not, some people are preparing for this second Civil War. They plan to do anything Trump, or whoever succeeds him, tells them to do to help him overthrow our democratic republic. In sheer numbers, they create a problem, just like Hitler's "Brown Shirts" of the 1930s in Germany.

Democracies may be more fragile than we had thought. If Trump is gone, Florida Governor Ron DeSantis and others have clarified that they are ready and willing to fill Trump's shoes. The end of Trump will not signal the end of the fascist movement in America. Several prominent senators and governors are all jockeying positions to take this mantle and go forward should Trump fall out of favor. Some may end up being far more dangerous than Trump.

Before WWII, people didn't think Hitler would accomplish much of anything because they knew he was an unintelligent, verbose fool. Even in Germany, he was seen as a fool and almost entirely out of touch with political, social, and economic reality. People on the streets would joke about him. They became accustomed to his hateful speeches and constant insults to anyone who disagreed with him. He never debated anything or anyone; he just attacked others with bombastic and utterly crazy and untrue statements and lies. His supporters ate it up, and most regular people laughed it off. Nothing was done to prepare for what was coming.

Hitler went on to try to fulfill his promise to restore Germany to its pre-WWI strength, but he ended up destroying much of Europe, causing the deaths of 60 million people. Then it was too late to start getting prepared.

If they had known all this would happen, rational Germans would have had weapons in advance, and the response would have been immediate and impactful. The Nazis might never have gotten much of a foothold in many occupied areas. They might never have gotten into power in Germany in the first place.

Hitler's Brownshirts were bullies when together with others. They got their way and intimidated voters, primarily by threatening and carrying weapons they seldom actually used in the early days beyond roughing people up. Once Hitler got 44% of the vote, he became Chancellor and got rid of the legislative branch of the German government. He and his supporters ended elections altogether, just as Trump's loyal "election deniers" are trying to do today in America.

Some Americans buying and "training" with their weapons are doing so today for similar purposes. It is a show of force that they are primarily working on. They feel that if they have enough guns, their opponents who see them will capitulate.

If enough people who support our democratic republic acquire and train with enough weapons, this becomes much less likely. The primary force to fight such a war is each state's National Guard, but ordinary citizens may also have to do so and become a resistance force to oppose a dictatorship if it comes to pass.

The concept here is making sure that a dictator never gets to consolidate power. An informed, determined, and suitably armed population can prevent that. What liberals, Democrats, and others need to ask is, are you okay with Trump-style supporters getting and keeping all the guns and ammunition? What could happen if you don't give it some thought? Safe and proper gun ownership by citizens concerned for our democratic republic can pose a significant deterrent to a dictator taking power here in the first place. Trump-type supporters are banking on your failure to consider this. Some people are now considering storing a weapon for such an event.

The "Stadtkirche" in Freudenstadt, destroyed in World War II, 1945, photo permission Stadtarchiv Freudenstadt, #2009020610044216.

CHAPTER TWO

THE NAZI SWINE

Some might think I overstate my concerns that Trumpism puts American democracy at risk. By extension, my statements about considering the use of the Second Amendment to protect our country against the possible threat of tyranny are overstated. Let me tell you a story that illustrates why and what I feel.

My wife and I recently dined with a dear friend who lives not far from us. Her name is Ingrid, and this is what she told us:

In 1941, Ingrid and her mother walked down Kopenicker Strasse (Street) in downtown Berlin, near their home. It was a bright but chilly day, so she wore her heavy coat to keep warm. As they returned home from shopping at a local store, two trucks stopped, one on either side of the street, and soldiers jumped out with guns. They began screaming and grabbing everyone wearing yellow stars on their coats and throwing them into the trucks. She was five years old, but the memory is so firmly seared into her mind that she can still remember it like it was yesterday. She will never forget that moment and the yellow cloth stars that Jews were required to wear on their clothing when they were out in public. Those victims were never seen again on the streets of Berlin.

She said that the soldiers allowed no discussion. They just grabbed people without warning. It happened so quickly that no one had a chance to resist. The sudden violence of this happening for the first, but not the last time, was stunning. No one could fight back. Those farther away fled as quickly as they could. People were scattering through the streets in every direction. She remembers that her mother grabbed her arm and ran, but her little legs could hardly keep up because her mother was pulling so hard and fast to escape. Ingrid was frightened because her grandfather was Jewish and had to wear the yellow star whenever he left their home. Ingrid's family feared that the Nazi soldiers would get them and that they would be exterminated. Even in 1941, many people in Germany were fully aware of the concentration camps and what was happening in them. Her grandfather had to live with Ingrid's family because Jews were not allowed houses or apartments.

One day at the beginning of 1944, the Nazis captured her grandfather and took him to a concentration camp where he was killed in the gas chambers. Her father was frightened. He knew it was only a matter of time before they would all be killed. He took his family on the next train to a town that was 440 miles to the west of Berlin in the Black Forest. It was a town called Freudenstadt. They left with just the clothes on their backs and had other property sent later by train.

Ingrid turned ten years old just before the end of WWII. She felt she had lived more than a lifetime under nationalist Nazi rule. Another vivid memory she told us was about walking home from school near the war's end when American pilots were bombing and strafing the railway yards in Freudenstadt. She said she could always hear the planes coming. She and her friends would jump into the ditch to avoid being hit by bullets. She said that the American fighters flew so low to the ground that she could see the faces of the pilots as they made their bombing and strafing runs down the road to the railway station. After the planes left, the children would return to the road and return to being kids again. They had become that accustomed to war.

As the Allies approached their town, the Nazis called the town together, gave everyone 13 or older a gun, and ordered them to fight for Hitler and his nationalist Nazi regime. As the American and French soldiers came near the town, they asked for the town to surrender so they could spare the life and property of everyone there. The Nazi soldiers refused and told the Americans that the citizens would all fight to the death. The Allies' artillery shelled the town for three days. It was destroyed. Ingrid and the survivors hid in a cave near town, and the Nazis still demanded that everyone die fighting for Hitler. The people had had enough and felt they would die anyway, so they just marched out of the cave together and surrendered to the Americans. The Nazi soldiers could not

GUN GUIDE FOR DEMOCRATS

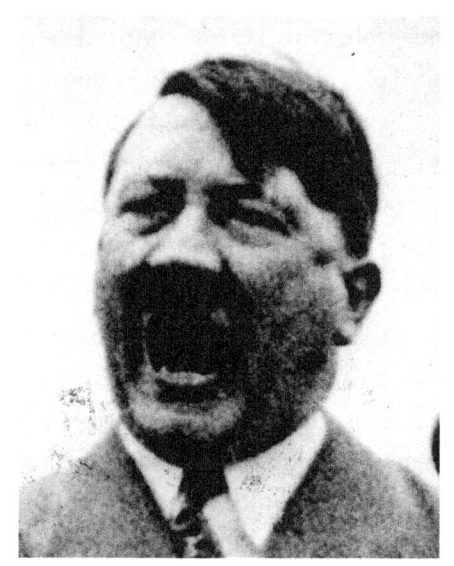

Adolf Hitler, August 5, 1939, Berlin, Germany, Keystone Pictures, Alamy Images.

Former President Trump, November 24, 2015, Myrtle Beach, South Carolina, Richard Ellis photo, Alamy Images.

stop and kill them all. This was the war's end for the people of Freudenstadt, and the Americans soon turned the captured town over to the French. Peace had finally come.

Ingrid was an outstanding student and happened to speak and write fluent French, English, and of course, German. Shortly after the war, she got a job as a translator for the US Army. She later met and married an American soldier. He took her back to the United States, where she has lived the rest of her life.

She knows first-hand what happened when Hitler told the German people that he would make Germany a great country again. She saw these policies in place when nationalism drove Germany's public outcry. She saw what happened when racial policies divided and attacked individual groups of citizens. She saw what happened when the citizens' voting rights were taken away.

She has also observed what has happened in America since Trump entered public politics. The speeches, attacks, and policies she sees are identical to those she heard from Hitler and the Nazi party in Germany in the 1930s and 1940s. I asked her what she thought of Trump, considering January 6, 2021. After thinking momentarily, she responded without a hit of irony: "Trump is a Nazi swine."

In the week before Christmas in 2021, a headline on CNN read, "Trump uses anti-Semitic tropes to criticize Jewish Americans again." He stated that Jewish Americans were disloyal to Israel and evangelical Christians in America. He said, "It's a very dangerous thing that's happening," when referring to American Jews. He called them out, not only for being Jewish but for being dangerous and disloyal. Similarly, on January 30, 1939, Hitler gave a national speech stating that Jews were dangerous to internal German security because of their inherent disloyalty. In 2017 after the Nazi and white supremacists rally in Charlottesville, Virginia, Trump said there were "Very fine people on both sides," to which Barack Obama responded, "How hard is it to say that Nazis are bad?" When Trump's insurrectionists and white supremacists attacked the capital on January 6th, he again called them "great people" and said he "loved" them.

Trump's own handpicked military Chief of Staff, General Mark Milley, compared the attack on our capital on January 6th to Hitler's 1933 attack on Germany's parliament building, which Hitler directed his supporters to carry out to justify his nationalist Nazi dictatorship taking complete power. Milley is quoted as saying, "This is a Reichstag moment," and called it, "The gospel of the Fuhrer." The Reichstag was the German national government building like our United States Capitol. Once it was destroyed,

Hitler became dictator, eliminated elections, and stopped counting votes, just like Trumpists tried to do on January 6th. Milley also stated that the supporters that Trump sent to destroy the capitol that day and to hang Vice-President Mike Pence and members of our Congress were the same as the "brownshirts in the streets" that Hitler had used at Nazi rallies. The "brown shirts" were the personal supporters of Hitler who went around Germany suppressing votes in elections, intimidating elected and government officials from counting legally cast votes, and terrifying citizens. They usually had banners, weapons, and flags to scare the population into accepting Hitler. With no one to stop them, Hitler took over.

It is essential to point out that most Germans were not members of the Nazi Party. Hitler's dictatorship did not represent most of the German people. Nazis ruled through terror and intimidation.

Ingrid told me her family story of the Holocaust must be told and re-told as often as possible so future generations might never forget those events. Her generation is passing away, but the stories of this terrible time should never be forgotten.

My friend Ingrid, along with many others, is convinced that America is living in troubling times and that what happened in Nazi Germany in her youth almost happened here in America on January 6th and still could happen if we are not vigilant.

CHAPTER THREE

THE SECOND AMENDMENT ISN'T JUST FOR REDNECKS

The Second Amendment to the U.S. Constitution says:

A well-regulated Militia, being necessary to the security of a free State, the right of the people to keep and bear Arms, shall not be infringed.

The Second Amendment is part of the Bill of Rights, the first ten amendments to the Constitution spelling out the rights of the citizens to keep their new government in check. The Second Amendment outlines the rights of citizens to protect themselves against tyranny.

For years, scholars debated whether the right to bear arms was a personal, individual right or whether it pertained only to the right to participate in a militia. In recent years, the Supreme Court has declared the right to be both individual and collective. Besides purchasing firearms for military service, purchasers may own firearms for personal protection, hunting, and recreation.

However, the Second Amendment is not absolute—for example, states may bar some people, such as felons or those committing domestic violence, from owning firearms. One of the most conservative justices on the United States Supreme Court, Justice Antonin Scalia, made this clear in a ruling on the Second Amendment.

Another federal law regulating firearms is the Brady Bill that Congress enacted after the assassination attempt against President Ronald Reagan. It requires licensed federal firearms dealers to hold a newly purchased weapon for a three-day cooling-off period while the dealer runs criminal records checks on the purchaser. That law also banned sales of certain "assault weapons," but that clause of the law has since expired.

A Republican political consultant in the Pacific Northwest where I live is a good friend. We agree on very few policies, but we have enjoyed the chess game of running campaigns against each other. Like us, political opponents in America need not be enemies, which we both believe. Some years ago, he told me that if liberals were right about Donald Trump and his desire to be a dictator, then I should be happy that the Second Amendment is there so we could restore our democracy. It seemed funny in 2015, but after January 6, 2021, it's not funny anymore.

Is a country more or less safe with firearms? Yes, no, and not necessarily. Nearly all citizens of Switzerland have been trained to use firearms to defend their country. They have very little crime, misuse, or improper discharge of firearms because of their regulations, education, and training. Their laws predominately pertain to acquiring, not owning firearms. No permit is necessary for just owning a firearm. A permit is necessary to buy semi and fully-automatic firearms. You do not need to list a reason for semi-automatic firearms purchases unless the purpose is other than sport-shooting, hunting, or collecting. Concealed carry permits are seldom allowed, as are permits for fully automatic weapons, silencers, and lasers. Hollow-point and soft-point ammunition may be sold over the counter for hunting only.

There is a long-standing practice of the Swiss participating in their national militia, and the Swiss keep these service rifles in their homes. The Swiss also have a strong hunting tradition, accounting for many firearms in the country. Before 2008, no firearms were even registered. In a 2019 referendum, Swiss voters opted to conform with European Union regulations restricting semi-automatic firearms acquisition with high-capacity magazines. However, citizens can obtain one of these permits if they promise they will show after five and ten years that they're members of a shooting club or that they used the weapon at least once a year within that five- and ten-year period.

In 2017 we had 39,773 firearm deaths in America, roughly one in 8,000, while Switzerland only had 214, or roughly one in 40,000. The problem is more about how Americans possess guns than the fact that they do so.

If you assert your Second Amendment right to own a firearm, you can also choose to be a responsible gun owner. There is little reason that your firearm should ever fall into the hands of criminals or be misused by others in your home or community.

Some extreme conservatives have told me that African Americans with firearms, especially AR-15s, are terrorists. This book is a bad idea because it teaches people they think should not possess guns about acquiring, possessing, and using guns. However, even though there has been staggering racial repression in America against minority communities over the decades, our Constitution's basic protections and promises apply to all American citizens equally, not just to conservative rednecks.

"Kill Jews" painted on a rock at a National Forest shooting location.

CHAPTER FOUR

WHO IS BUYING GUNS NOW, AND WHY?

Some years ago, a news story indicated almost as many guns in America as Americans. That was a big story then, and today the number is higher. Although there is no way to know, most experts agree that there are around 1.2 guns per person in our country, or roughly 400 million.

There was a significant upswing in purchases of guns and ammunition after the election of President Obama. Conservatives were concerned that he would attempt gun control. They bought so much ammunition that local Walmarts could not keep up with their customers' demand for ammo, even small caliber .22 shells. This panic tapered off over time. Alarmists failed to realize that President Obama was a trained Constitutional lawyer who knew the status of Second Amendment law.

The Supreme Court decision of *District of Columbia v. Heller* was announced in June 2008, six months before Obama took office. Before that time, the Court had not considered the ultimate question, "Is the right to bear arms an individual right?" Historically, the NRA and guns rights proponents didn't bring the case to court for fear that the Supreme Court of the United States would hold that the Second Amendment did NOT create an individual right to own firearms. No gun control advocates filed the case for fear that the Court would hold that individual ownership WAS an individual right.

As a Constitutional Law professor, Obama undoubtedly was aware of this historical stand-off. Although there was panic buying of firearms and ammunition when he was elected, Obama did not promise or attempt to act on guns until he wept over the slaughter of the 6-year-olds at Sandy Hook and said, in essence, "Something should be done." Still, he never proposed any attempt to repeal the Second Amendment.

When Trump was elected, a rush to purchase firearms began again. This corresponded to an explosion in purchasing "military-style assault weapons" (More on these firearms in a later chapter). There were three reasons for this. First, a 10-year ban on sales of "assault weapons," enacted under President Reagan in 1994, had expired. Although it was debated at length, Congress did not reinstate the ban, so assault-style weapons became widely available. Second, people noticed these types of weapons and thought they were cool. Frequently, these weapons were purchased by poorly trained people who knew little about them, often by young white men.

Third, there were purchases by conservative Trumpists who "trained" with these weapons for what they saw as the coming second American Civil War. They are convinced that liberals, Democrats, and communities of color will never consider doing anything similar, so they will receive a complete and quick surrender when they do take over. Their concept isn't so much to use firearms in combat as to use them to intimidate others into a quick political result.

You might wonder how Trump supporters responded immediately after the insurrection on January 6, 2021. FBI data can give a bit of a look into the overall American response. Federal firearms background checks for gun purchases jumped 40% from 2020 to 12,452,319 checks in the first quarter of 2021. Many purchases these days are not reported, and these checks were not made, so not all purchases are reflected in these numbers. This increase coincided with a significant shortage of ammunition on store shelves, especially for ammunition that can be fired from military assault-style weapons like AR-15s. Even today, some store shelves are bare, and larger stores have limited the number of boxes customers may buy during one visit. Recently, the national outdoor retailer Bass Pro limited customers to 5 boxes of this type of ammunition when available. A box contains 20 rounds (bullets). Equally impactful is the cost. Not long ago, these rounds cost roughly $.30 each, but now usually sell for over a dollar, even for poor-quality bullets made in Russia or China.

Atomwaffen Division members in the forests of Washington State with their firearms.

American manufacturers make over 12 billion rounds of ammunition per year, so this is not a supply chain or scarcity issue. This is consumer-driven by people hoarding bullets and preparing for political and civil strife in America. This is not an overstatement. In March 2019, U.S. Representative Steve King, R-Iowa, posted a meme about a hypothetical civil war between "blue states" and "red states." The since-deleted post was an image of two figures composed of traditionally Democratic-leaning and Republican-leaning states in fighting postures with text over the top and a caption that read: "Folks keep talking about another civil war. One side has about 8 trillion bullets, while the other doesn't know which bathroom to use."

This is not about shadowy messages hidden deep on the internet or elsewhere. A sitting United States Congressman publicly stated that he and his supporters were buying and storing bullets to kill Americans who disagreed. This second American Civil War would usher in a Trumpian dictatorship and the end of our democratic republic. In 2018, when King's white supremacist views were widely known, Trump campaigned with King and proudly said to a cheering crowd, "[King] may be the world's most conservative human being." Trump boasted that he had raised more campaign money for King than any other candidate that year. Fortunately, King was opposed by the Republican party and lost his primary in 2020. He is no longer in Congress, but his views represent some Americans' feelings.

Moving forward, something entirely new is happening in America. The other day I ran into a good friend I hadn't seen in a while due to the pandemic. This woman and her husband are very progressive liberals. Both are college-educated, and she is a lawyer. As we were talking and catching up, I mentioned this book. After about five minutes, she returned to the book's subject and said sheepishly that they both had bought guns for themselves. Being surprised and curious, I asked why. She told me it was a direct response to January 6, 2021, and the rise of Trumpism. Another progressive liberal neighbor told me in February of 2022 that she plans to get an AR-15 soon for the same reason.

This perceived threat from the events surrounding January 6, 2021, is beginning to drive a new group of gun buyers in America to do more than just plan but also purchase firearms.

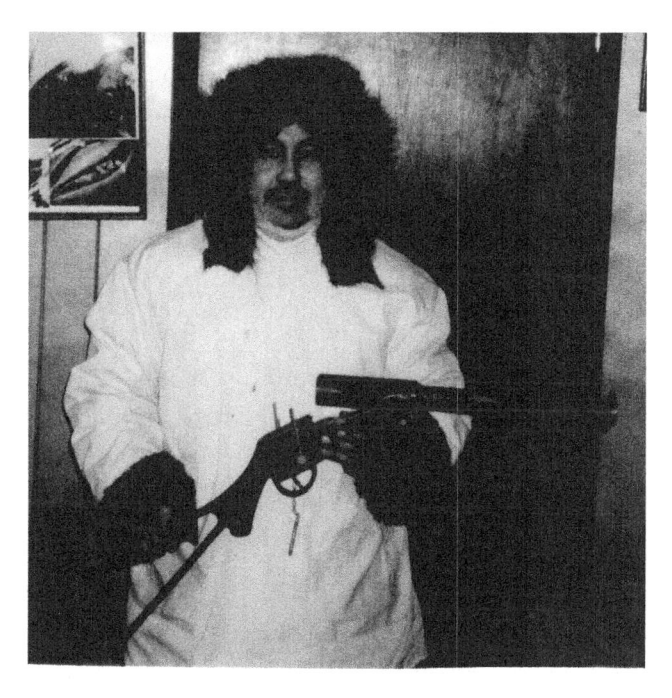

My friend Tommy Agiak in Kaktovik, Alaska, with a whale gun in 1984.

CHAPTER FIVE

A BRIEF HISTORY OF FIREARMS

There is a fascinating principle in law called "Inevitable discovery." Simplified, evidence discovered illegally can still be used against an accused criminal in a trial if it had been lawfully found someday. An example is a dead body. A dead body will be discovered eventually, even if it is found illegally, say during police entry into a building with a warrant that turns out to be defective. Things that will be found anyway are a reality, so society must address them. We can't wish them away or pretend they do not exist.

Discoveries in science will inevitably be found as well. For better or worse, humans were always going to discover subatomic particles and, in so doing, make atomic bombs and blow each other up. It was always going to happen. Throughout history, people have made discoveries that help them survive and live better, but they also have found ways to turn discoveries into weapons.

In roughly the ninth century, Chinese chemists mixed sulfur, charcoal, and saltpeter and found that when ignited, it blew up. This was early gunpowder, which made fantastic fireworks after it was discovered. Then someone wondered what would happen if you compressed that explosion in a tube, added fragments of hard material, and shot it at someone else. Although crude, it was a firearm. Millions of people have been shot since then by all manner of gunpowder devices. It would have been nice if we had just stopped at the fireworks, but human history has often been violent.

As technology advances, most inventions are succeeded by something new, but a few things never change much. Gunpower is one of them. Even modern explosives have not replaced age-old gunpowder in some of the most modern personal firearms.

Firearms did not create wars, but they did make them less personal. Shooting someone a long distance off was much different from stabbing someone with a sword. Dropping bombs or shooting a cannon at others differs from using a spear. Humans created efficiencies but also lessened the personal courage necessary for combatants.

Some cultures, like the Samurai of ancient Japan, resisted these new modern weapons because they felt that more distant killing

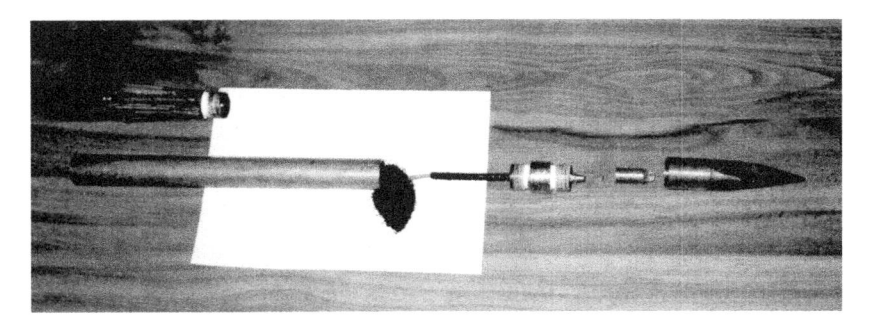

A whale gun fires this explosive bullet.

was not honorable. It's an interesting point. How many large wars would have been fought if the leaders and their families were required to be on the front lines of personal combat?

What was once primarily a product for war also became helpful in hunting. It's safer to kill a deer or a bear with a firearm than a spear, which made feeding a family easier before supermarkets.

Not long ago, Americans hunted with rifles or shotguns to put food on their tables. Some still do. Hunting for food requires some personal responsibility in harvesting it. It was not uncommon for some native cultures to return the hooves and bones of harvested creatures to the forest to show their thanks and to prove that they had not wasted any of it. Such was the respect and obligation people felt when they were in tune with nature, a healthy process, and firearms were a part of it. Respectful and responsible hunting in America remains a part of our national history and culture.

When the Second Amendment was enacted, the firearms available for personal and military use were not even a fraction as powerful, accurate, or complex as the ones on the market today. The muskets used in the American Revolution were highly inaccurate smooth-bore long guns. The rifling inside the barrels of guns (the valleys and ridges) made them much more accurate and didn't become widely used until the 1800s. That was the dawn of modern firearms.

Most modern firearms today are lighter and far more accurate than older ones. Some can hold many bullets rather than just one. Others can automatically fire and reload bullets into their firing chambers, allowing the shooter to fire many bullets per second. Semi-automatic and fully automatic firearms are widely available in America today, and many are in the hands of people with no practical use or training. For these owners, their guns are more of a status symbol or political statement than a self-defense or hunting tool. Most of them are unsuitable for hunting because they do too much damage to the meat or are far too inaccurate.

Recent American history of firearms saw social and political developments as well. In editing this book, a friend reminded me of a scene in a movie where the hero breaks into the wrong hotel room, one full of people. Everyone inside pulls out a gun and aims it at the hero simultaneously. The hero responds, "Oh, Americans." That is how the world sees Americans; honestly, it's how we see ourselves. Current movies contain a staggering amount of gun violence, and that trend is increasing. We know this part of our image is an accurate assessment. Right or wrong, being the toughest kid on the block is part of being an American. Weapons and our military are part of how we project power on the world stage. You can no longer separate America and our culture of guns.

As our political and social climate changed in the last 50 years, average Americans began buying guns for purposes other than hunting or sporting. Gun sales also exploded in a way unseen in our past. Since over 80% of the guns in the United States are manufactured here, gun production is a reasonable indicator of the available guns. The following data is from a U.S. Department of Justice Office of Justice Programs July 1995 report:

From 1973 to 1993, according to Bureau of Alcohol, Tobacco, and Firearms (ATF) data, U.S. manufacturers produced the following handguns alone:

6.6 million .357 Magnum revolvers
6.5 million .38 Special revolvers
5.4 million .22 caliber pistols
5.3 million .22 caliber revolvers
4.5 million .25 caliber pistols
3.1 million 9-millimeter pistols
2.4 million .380 caliber pistols
2.2 million .44 Magnum revolvers
1.7 million .45 caliber pistols
1.2 million .32 caliber revolvers

The ATF estimates that from 1899 to 1993, about 223 million guns became available in the United States, including over 79 million rifles, 77 million handguns, and 66 million shotguns. The number of guns seized, destroyed, lost, or not working is unknown. The number of new handguns added to those available has exceeded the number of new shotguns and rifles in recent years. More than half of the guns added in 1993 were handguns.

According to this FBI data, since the mid-1990s, the U.S. civilian gun inventory has increased from around 192 million, roughly 64 million handguns, to 265 million firearms, including 112 million handguns. By 2015, Americans owned more firearms; some owned both handguns and long guns. Around 10 percent of owners had ten or more firearms, almost 40 percent of all guns. Seventy million firearms changed hands between buyers from 2011 to 2015. Two and a half percent of Americans had guns stolen from 2010 to 2015, accounting for an estimated five hundred thousand guns getting into the hands of criminals.

This dynamic has changed dramatically since that last report. Handguns were the main topic as their sales exploded in America. It was easy to see that much of this resulted from citizens responding to real or imagined fear of being crime victims. In recent years, politics has become a driving factor. As people now arm themselves for civil strife, the move has been towards high-capacity military assault-style firearms. It is difficult to get accurate, current data on this trend because so many sales have gone unreported through purchases at gun shows, private sales, and online purchases. Unfortunately, some data on this purchase explosion exists only partly and is anecdotal. The other problem with data in the last decade is that the FBI and ATF need more time to compile and analyze what has happened with these off-the-books sales between individuals who bypass the existing gun purchase rules.

The military has developed many hand-held firearms that can fire exploding shells, some that can even stop a tank. These can be laser-guided or "wire-guided," in which a spool of wire shoots out with the projectile, allowing the shooter to modify where the projectile goes by moving the wire.

Other historical developments in firearms have included advances in ammunition. There are exploding or burning rounds that were developed for particular purposes. Some firearms have burning bullets to show the shooter where the bullet goes during flight. These bullets, called tracers, are used predominately by the military, but private citizens also use them.

I have seen another example of a particular weapon while working as a police officer in Barrow, Alaska. Native hunters used bullets called "whale bombs" fired from a whale gun. These date from the late 19th century, but Inuit Eskimos hunting Bowhead whales in the Arctic still use them today. The gun is heavy and made of brass, like an old-fashioned cannon. It is a shoulder-fired weapon. After harpooning a whale, hunters pull in the rope attached to the harpoon, and once they have pulled their walrus-skin boat alongside the whale, they shoot the whale. The bullet, or bomb, goes into the whale, exploding a huge amount of black powder. Thousands of copper shrapnel pieces from the bullet quickly go through and kill the whale, allowing the hunters to harvest it more humanely and reduce the danger to the Inuit hunters maneuvering in the freezing waters of the Arctic Ocean.

The last feature defining modern firearms is the design of the brass casing that holds the bullet and the gunpowder itself. New versions make bullets faster and more efficient than older ones. Shotguns that used to have paper shells, which some still do, have been replaced mainly by plastic ones. There are also bullet cases now made of aluminum and steel instead of brass. Steel is commonly used in Russian and Chinese ammunition to save on costs. These new cases also contain bullets with new and improved ballistic performance, which we discuss in the chapter "How a Bullet Works."

.50 caliber weapons were once only for the military, but citizens can buy some of them today.

CHAPTER SIX

HOW ACCURATE ARE GUNS?

Any firearm can be deadly. Some are more precise instruments than others, but the key to accuracy is the operator. In a later chapter, we will discuss certain firearms and calibers for different uses in more detail.

How accurate is any firearm? Like every question in this book, the answer is – "It depends." A gun is a machine, and like every other machine, there are good and bad ones. Some are worthless; no matter who uses them, they are not and will never be reliable or accurate. They have flawed designs, or they are manufactured poorly. On the other hand, there are well-made and reliable firearms that work perfectly and would be highly accurate but haven't hit that proverbial "broad side of a barn door" because of operator error.

Reliability, safety, capacity, and accuracy are four basic concepts when evaluating firearms. Americans are told that everything is all about capacity. Bigger with more bullets always seems to be better, and why not? Isn't it better to have 30 or 40 bullets than six? Not if you can't hit anything with them if the gun does not fire, or if you do not know how to use it. Any gunfight against another person that is not over after the first or second bullet is one you will probably lose.

Do not think more complex or faster-firing guns are always the best. They often are not at all, and many faster, more popular, or more complex guns are notoriously inaccurate and prone to malfunction. Many popular military assault-style firearms are primarily offensive weapons intended to spray bullets rather than to aim precisely and are poor defensive weapons in most situations, like in your home for self-defense. These are commonly marketed to young men, untrained in their tactical use, who see them as an extension of their manhood. Gun manufacturer Remington advertised these weapons with an ad campaign that said, "Get Your Man Card Back!" The Sandy Hook mass murderer used one of these weapons. He did not need to be accurate with one of these weapons against many people in a small, confined space.

On May 17, 2015, there was a shootout in Waco, Texas, at the Twin Peaks Restaurant involving over 200 participants, most of them members of motorcycle gangs. Police later recovered 320 weapons from the crime scene, many automatic or military assault-style rifles, like AK-47s. The police responded, and they also had automatic military assault rifles. When the shootout was over, only nine persons were killed. Eighteen were wounded. One hundred seventy-seven people were arrested. One might think that outlaw motorcycle gang members with automatic weapons, engaged in an all-out gunfight lasting for quite a while, starting in a restaurant, and spilling out onto its parking lot, might end up with most people dead. Still, even people who carry guns regularly are not necessarily good at using them to shoot others. In a later chapter, we will discuss killing people in more detail and why it is more challenging than most people understand.

On February 7, 2022, an intriguing headline in the Seattle Times announced that there had been a gunfight on the streets of a neighborhood at 2:30 in the morning. Witnesses reported that many people were involved in the shootout. After the shootout, suspects were seen fleeing on foot and in vehicles. When the police arrived, they found bullets all around the neighborhood. Bullets had hit houses, businesses, and cars. Police recovered dozens of bullet cases from the scene, not including any fired from inside the vehicles that had fled the area. What police did not find was any indication that anyone had been shot. Why? Once again, because of the operators.

In the third example of accuracy, I was on duty one day when a call occurred, reporting a shooting in progress. I was the first officer to arrive at the scene but missed the bad guys by about a minute. Other officers arrived, and we received reports of events related to this crime scene showing up in other locations. A vehicle crashed into the side of the road a few miles away. That car hit an embankment, seriously injuring two young men. The driver did more than miss a turn—he was bleeding from a gunshot wound and lost consciousness. Besides being injured in the crash, the passenger had his spine severed near his hips by a bullet from a .308 hunting rifle that passed through him and into the driver.

You must excuse me, but the crime scene at the victim's home amused me. Bullet casings lay everywhere - - in the house, on the porch, in the driveway, in the yard. It looked like the shootout at the OK Corral. But no bodies could be seen, nor even a drop of blood. The incident started as a purchase of $170 worth of marijuana. However, the bad guys didn't have $170. What they did have were guns. So, of course, being bad guys, it made sense to them to pull out their guns and rob the seller. What could go wrong? The marijuana-buying bad guys had a Mac-10, which resembles a small hand-held submachine gun that you might see in a James Bond movie, plus a 9mm automatic handgun with extra ammunition clips, just in case.

The drugs were displayed, and the guns came out - - all within 10 feet of one another - - but unfortunately for the "buyers," the seller also had a 9mm automatic handgun with several clips of ammunition because you never know what to expect with drug customers. He pulled out his gun, and the bullets began to fly. They shot at each other throughout the house with semi-automatic firearms. The gunfight spilled out onto the porch. They shot at each other in the yard and the driveway, reloading and leaving shell casings as the robbers fled to their vehicle.

The buyers realized they were never going to get the marijuana. They got to their vehicle just as the seller ran out of bullets for his automatic handgun. He returned to the house and retrieved a single-shot bolt-action .308 hunting rifle. As the buyers tried to drive away from the house, the seller shot a single bullet into the vehicle. It pierced the passenger door, severed the passenger's spine, and struck the driver.

The seller was never charged for the attempted drug sale or for shooting the buyers. The prosecutor deemed it a case of self-defense, although chasing after the fleeing would-be robbers might have well exceeded any right of self-defense. The buyers, including the paraplegic who is now in a wheelchair for the rest of his life, are serving most of their lives in prison due to this incident and their extensive criminal histories.

This incident demonstrates two essential points. First, bringing or displaying a gun in most situations is a terrible idea. Second, guns, especially automatic weapons in the wrong hands, are almost hopelessly inaccurate. Most people with automatic weapons will begin firing wildly because they have so many bullets to use up. They rely on these extra bullets to compensate for bad placement and poor tactical techniques.

A mental state also makes some people tactically incompetent, no matter how many bullets they have or how quickly their gun can fire. The faster they fire, the worse their shooting gets. This is partly because most Americans with firearms have no training, knowledge, preparation, or ability to bring them to a gunfight.

Owning a gun and shooting at a range or in the forest does little to prepare a person for using firearms tactically. Many people with firearms in America can never learn tactical skills.

Imagine a gunfight with just one person as your opponent, no matter how that person is armed. With any decently made firearm, the accuracy in an armed conflict is determined by the intelligence, discipline, and training for such a situation; even then, shooting to kill will be difficult. The gunfight should be over after the first shot or two. After that, it becomes the OK Corral, and it's just up to luck.

Guns are not inherently accurate or inaccurate in and of themselves. Competence, preparation, intelligence, and courage are human traits. The size or capacity of the gun you buy will not replace or augment these.

CHAPTER SEVEN

KILLING PEOPLE

As an experienced lawman, Wyatt Earp seldom carried a firearm on duty. That was not uncommon in the old West. Old-timers out west did not carry handguns often; they were cowboys, ranchers, and farmers with gardens and cattle to tend to if they wanted to eat. If cowboys on horses had carried handguns constantly, you would find them on the ground all over the western plains and grasslands with rusted-out tin cans, wheel rims, and other waste from old-time settlements. They used rifles, not pistols, to kill predators, hunt, and fight wars. But unlike depictions in the movies, most people weren't packing heat. Most early American towns out west prohibited firearms from being taken into their jurisdictional limits because people drank alcohol in bars and other recreational establishments. In the 1800s, major Western towns like Tombstone, Deadwood, and Dodge City had some of America's most restrictive gun laws, far more restrictive than today. By most estimates, fewer than 10% of Americans in frontier areas ever carried handguns. The common misconception that the conservative mantra of "God, guns, and guts" in the Old West made America is Hollywood fiction. Hardworking and industrious Americas built this country, but they were seldom armed.

Many police officers around the world today do not carry guns. They believe most people will not shoot an unarmed person, especially a police officer. Having or displaying a gun changes the dynamics in all conflicts, even for law enforcement officers. Don't get me wrong, police carry weapons of different types and need to use them sometimes, especially in America, but not as often as you might think. Few officers will kill a person in their careers with a service weapon. Pew Research Data reported in February 2017 that 83% of Americans think police fire their weapons while on duty. Many believe they fire them more than once annually—only about one-quarter of police fire weapons at another person in their entire career. Male police officers fire their weapons at other people thrice as often as female officers (30% to 11%). White officers fire their weapons a third more often (31% to 21%) than non-white officers, and officers with military backgrounds discharge their weapons at others more often than those without military backgrounds (32% to 26%).

Some Americans have acquired guns in hopes that guns would make them seem, or even be, more powerful or dangerous than they are. This is part of American gun culture, but guns can't solve problems, especially for someone who is neither brave nor dangerous, and they can often make things worse.

If you had a firearm, could you pull the trigger? Some people could pull a trigger and kill you without batting an eye. Others could never do it. How can you tell?

As you would expect, the armed people I have faced in my career presented varying degrees of risk. Some were making a statement not associated with the gun at all. Many were drunk and could not pose a great risk, so long as I had some cover while implementing a better plan. Frankly, some police shootings have happened because the officers exposed themselves to risk unnecessarily and then had to shoot to protect themselves. This is not necessarily a "bad" shooting in the sense of being legally unjustified, but other options were available with proper cover. "Cover" means hiding behind something, anything really, that a person cannot shoot through or can't see you through.

Part 1 of 5 – Dangerous People & Killing
In police work, you meet people who are dangerous because they are drunk or on drugs, and sometimes people who are cold-hearted killers. I have been faced with people pointing a gun at me many times. In one case, I was called to a domestic disturbance at a house in Barrow, Alaska. A drunk teenage girl had warrants for her arrest, and her family wanted her taken away. Her room was at the end of a hallway. She had pulled a short dresser to block the doorway, and as I approached, she was closing the bolt of a hunting rifle. I drew my service revolver, tightening my grip on the trigger and taking aim when the family began screaming at me not to shoot her, "It's okay! She won't shoot you!" As I moved backward, I told them, "Okay, then you will take the gun away from her." I was locked into the process of killing her and was only waiting for the barrel of her rifle to come up and get close to leveling on me, and then, I would shoot. The family burst past me, and they took the gun from her. She had only delayed shooting me because she could not close the breach. After all, she was trying to load the rifle with the wrong size of ammunition.

That was a close call, and I think that if she could have, she would have shot me, but she didn't, mostly because she was drunk. Few sober and rational people would try that unless they were trying to commit suicide by cop, which is a real thing. I am happy that I did not have to kill this teenage girl in front of her family. Things are often confusing and complex in situations like that.

Another time I was with an officer on duty. I was in plain clothes setting up an electronic surveillance device that I had placed on a car. I was not armed then because I'd been crawling under cars getting the system set up and working, and I didn't want to lose or damage my handgun in the tight space under the car. To test the device, another officer and I hopped into an unmarked car and drove up and down the highway to calibrate the signal for use the next day. Suddenly, a truck passed us at high speed and skidded to a stop sideways in front of us, blocking the highway. A guy jumped out, aimed a handgun at us, and said, "Out of the car motherfuckers!" This came as a big surprise to us. I opened my door and dropped to the ground behind the door. My partner opened his door and, with the door as cover, announced us as police officers. He let the guy know he was the one who was about to die, not us. In just that fraction of a second, we could see that the driver was drunk, confused, and unconfident in his actions. My partner did not shoot, and the bad guy slowly lowered his gun.

We handcuffed him and asked him what he was doing. He said he had been drinking at the bar and heard that someone was letting the air out of tires on parked cars, so he was trying to find who was doing it. We booked him for second-degree assault.

Later, my partner almost quit police work because he felt he had failed a severe test many officers may face in their careers: should he have shot a person? Even now, I can't tell you whether I would have shot the guy if I had been armed. It's hard to second-guess these things. And yes, I know I should have been carrying a gun, but these things also happen sometimes. I urged my partner to consider that he might have made a good decision and that the risk was not as bad as it seemed, considering that he also had cover. (The bad guy died two years later when he drove that same truck, drunk on his ass, rolled it over, didn't have a seat belt on, and got crushed to death after falling halfway out the window.) In my partner's case, I think that his decision at the time was the correct answer. He stayed in police work and had an outstanding career as one of the best homicide detectives I had ever met.

Judging risk is part of any armed encounter. A trained, experienced police officer has both a practical and legal advantage in a shooting situation that a private citizen does not.

Some people are dangerous, and you can feel it. On another occasion, I was part of an undercover bust of a cocaine dealer, and the electronic bust signal went wrong. This can happen anytime radios are used. I got stuck, without cover, out in the open, only 20 feet from the bad guy who had his back to me. He was wearing a long black leather jacket. I aimed my gun at him, near his heart-lung area, just below his shoulders, and identified myself as a police officer, but the rest of the bust team slowly arrived. He looked over his shoulder and could see it was only me. He slowly looked over his shoulder with his right hand inside his left breast jacket pocket. He looked at me and then looked forward. He looked back again and right at my eyes. I instantly felt he had a gun and was planning to kill me. I steadied my aim and tightened the trigger as I slowly exhaled to take the anticipated shot if I saw him turn with a gun to fire. He saw this and finally said, "Okay. Okay." He slowly took his hand off the gun I had not seen and raised his hands. He announced that he had a gun to keep everything safe. My partners showed up, and we took him into custody.

He was as cool as a cucumber. I asked him what he was thinking, and he told me he was planning to kill me, and in most cases, he would have, but when he looked back the second time, he could sense that I was in the process of shooting him and decided by the look in my eye that I would do it. He was right. I could also see this in him. He said that he could probably turn and shoot a cop before he or she ever fired a weapon. This is a pretty good assessment most of the time.

This guy was a cold, calculating killer, and he didn't seem like his pulse rate went up. This is what dangerous people are like. They will not threaten you. They will not display a gun in advance. They will not tell you that they have a gun. They will not act like a tough guy or say anything at all. They don't have to. A perilous person does not need to try to convince you of it. It is part of the talkers-seldom-do and doers-seldom-talk thing. People who open-carry or wear guns out in public, screamers, and protesters with military-style firearms and flags running around the streets are not the people you need to worry about. They are the talkers. They are generally just fools. Actual dangerous people never do silly things like that.

Part 2 of 5 – Courage (or Nerve) Under Fire

I have a few stories illuminating some mental aspects of how you will feel the first time a person points a gun at you and some common psychological responses. Everyone will be different, but you should consider all these if you plan to arm yourself with a gun. Remember that if someone does point a gun at you, or you point one at someone else, either of you is possibly very close to the last few moments of your life. Everything will change in those moments. You will need to be prepared.

Some years ago, I attended a training class in California on what in police work we call "Red Flag" events. These deadly encounters happened because the officers or detectives ignored or did not see warnings along the way that led up to bad events. Working undercover for many years, I saw many bad, complicated, unpleasant, and unplanned things happen. We often missed signs or indicators along the way that made things worse. Sometimes technological problems come from our carelessness. Inattention made these situations worse. Not correctly checking a battery in a transmitter before an undercover operation is a great example.

The instructor told a story of an undercover bust that he was involved in that went bad. He used the code word for the arrest team to come to his aid. Unfortunately, the arrest team did not hear the signal, and the bad guy pushed the detective to the floor, pulled out his gun, and pulled the trigger. The automatic handgun misfired. He racked another round into the chamber. He pulled the trigger, and it misfired again. After the third misfire, which happened in a few seconds, the detective could grab the bad guy, and as they struggled on the floor, the arrest team in the next room heard the noise, came in, and saved the day.

As this detective told the story about the moments in which he was sure that he was going to die, I could sense something in his voice and demeanor. He was struggling to express something difficult to say or convey. I felt a chill come over me. He was speaking in a language that I understood. During the break, I approached him to talk about a movie I once saw. Before I could even say the movie's name, he said, "I know; I watch it repeatedly." The movie was "Fearless" starring Jeff Bridges, which expresses the experience of being so near death and then surviving. A 1993 newspaper reviewer in the *Seattle Times* called the movie "Emotionally devastating." The movie captures this moment in a way I have seldom seen expressed in any medium. Watching it seems to help some people relive a traumatic moment and heal over time.

Three times in my life, I was in situations where, like that instructor, I was entirely sure my life was over. Although I have had people point guns at me in my police career, none of my three events involved firearms. I always felt that I was in control of the firearm encounters, but once I was lost in a storm on the ice in the Arctic Ocean in the winter; on another occasion, the engine of my airplane quit in the dark at a low altitude, and I once had a work-related medical emergency in which my heart stopped beating for a couple of minutes, but I stayed awake. In these three events, there seemed to be no way out. I entered a mental state where everything went into slow motion, and milliseconds seemed to last hours. I was not overly frightened then, and my actions remained deliberate and controlled. I felt my life had ended - like I was merely an observer. I can resurrect that state of mind in a stressful situation. I would stay calm during the event, but the fear would come later, usually in a few days. This won't be easy to understand if you have not had such an experience. If you survive one, and your fear comes later, that cannot be easy to deal with. That is one effect of post-traumatic stress disorder that a shooting or other near-death situation can cause.

Some people find themselves in such mental clarity when they enter a deadly shooting situation. I always have, and I do not know why for sure. Sometimes I feel like things are slowing down, and an odd sense of calm. Others do not respond this way at all and entirely fall apart. Once, I was working with a new police officer, and we were waiting outside a house to arrest the suspect in a planned mass shooting at a school. After the arrest, we would do a search warrant on his residence. The officer leaned over to me in the bushes outside the house in the dark and said, "I think I am going to piss my pants." Although I appreciated his candor, this is not what I wanted to hear from a fellow police officer in such a situation. Our team debriefed the event later, as usual, and after a long discussion, we all concluded that this was not the right line of work for him. He resigned from his commission and moved on to another life outside police work.

These are examples of how you might act or respond when faced with a deadly encounter. This is just a warning to consider how you might experience a tactical situation. It could influence your buying and displaying a weapon against another person.

Courage (nerve) never comes from your firearm in a firefight. It does not come from the number of bullets in your gun or how cool your gun looks in person, online, or in a YouTube video. Although it is acceptable to be afraid, discipline, intelligence, and planning create the poise that protects someone in a gunfight. Firepower, flags, slogans, or ostentatious displays of military-style weapons in public demonstrations cannot replace this.

Part 3 of 5 – Killing in Combat – More Difficult Than You Think
A fascinating statistic arose during WWI among fighter pilots. Only 15% of the pilots accounted for most aerial kills (enemy airplanes being shot down). Initially, it was surmised that some pilots were better pilots and better shots. Still, many pilots engaged in significant "dog fights" or aerial combat with enemy fighters but did not fire their guns or only fired them when no one was near where the bullets might hit.

Infantry soldiers had even worse results. Most would return from combat without having fired any bullets from their weapons. Soldiers were observed shooting above or away from the enemy. Some political and military leaders without combat experience were confounded. They failed to understand fundamental human nature, which they, as non-combatants, usually knew nothing about. By WWII, only 15% to 20% of soldiers were willing to fire their weapons in combat. Even fewer were willing to kill another person intentionally. Tactical encounters and war, up close and personal, are very different from what John Wayne made it look like in the movies.

In truth, most people will not, or cannot, shoot or kill another person without significant training. If it were easy to do, there would be few of us left in the world. Although people get shot and killed daily in America, it is usually drunk, mentally ill, deranged, or psychotic people who shoot and kill others. Criminally psychotic people (only roughly 1% of the general population has this designation, and few kill others) tend to be attracted to crime, killing, and gangs. These people are not ordinary in society, even though media stories sometimes make us think they are everywhere.

Battle-hardened gang members conduct a significant number of the shootings that occur in larger American cities. You are not likely to encounter or be assaulted by them in your home unless you live right in their neighborhood. Even then, most of their shootings and killings occur within their organizations or between their members and rival gangs.

The problem for governments during wartime was getting soldiers to shoot their opponents. Leaders began to realize that the best way to do this was to objectify a person's opponent. If a soldier could not kill another person, it might be easier if he did not think of the other soldier as a person. Japanese became "nips," and Germans became "krauts." Opponents were portrayed as baby killers who raped women when they conquered territories. All sides of conflicts did this to motivate their soldiers. Not only were soldiers more willing to kill their opponents, but it also made war crimes and other abuses more likely and common. Unfortunately, the two went hand in hand.

I met a man once whose life exemplifies the effectiveness of objectifying an enemy. My friend Bernie Wemmer and I were part-time flight instructors in our spare time. Bernie's older brother, Reinhard Wemmer, was also a pilot, and he went flying with us one day some years ago. Reinhard was much older than we were and had been a pilot in WWII in Germany. He showed us his logbook filled with German writing and swastika stamps. He was trained to fly the Messerschmitt 109, but at the end of his training, Germany ran out of aviation fuel for its fighter aircraft and was put into the infantry. His first battle was the Battle of the Bulge, very near the end of WWII. He was severely wounded and was left on the battlefield to die. He had been told that if Americans captured him, they would torture and eat him. He was wholly convinced by nationalist Nazi propaganda that Americans were cannibals. He told me he believed this was true because indoctrination and brainwashing were so intense in Germany. A dictatorial leadership culture based on a personality cult like Hitler's made this easy.

Reinhard Wemmer, severely wounded on the battlefield, was captured by the American soldiers and given medical help and a chocolate bar. He told me that he never forgot that moment on the battlefield. He resolved that if he lived, he wanted to move to America. He felt that any country that treated its prisoners of war in such a way was where he wanted to live and move his family. He survived and did as he promised on the battlefield that day.

The point here is to show governments' lengths to get soldiers to kill others. With new training and objectification of the enemy, shooting and killing rates rose to about 50% by the end of WWII. By the Korean War, that went up even higher. Not surprisingly, modern soldiers are de-sensitized to killing, and their weapons can kill at further distances, even by remote control. However, society does not want to create serial killers either. That is also a problem because many soldiers transition into civilian police work. Soldiers are not trained to be problem solvers, and conversely, civilian police departments are concerned with the militarization of their forces. It is a delicate balance.

Part 4 of 5 – Automatic Overload – Fast Firing Weapons

Firing a military-style automatic or semiautomatic firearm, spewing out multiple shots per second, does not solve the problem of a shooter's needing mental discipline and physical precision to kill in a home defense situation. Military assault-style firearms are not magic. They do not think or fire on their own. No one will know precisely what they will do in an armed encounter until they face one in person. A military assault-style rifle cannot lessen this reality. A person could go to gun ranges with an AR-15-style gun for a thousand years and shoot a thousand rounds daily, but the mental aspect of the first time facing a gun aimed at them will be complicated.

The other problem with fast-firing weapons, like an AR-15 or other military assault-style automatic firearms, is that the faster you fire, the more inaccurate you become. The noise and recoil will cause your heart and mind to race even more, and as you try to steady the impacts from the bullets, you fire more quickly to get your aim back, which does not work.

On March 19, 2022, a fight broke out between two persons at a car show and picnic in Dumas, Arkansas. As often happens with Americans, they pulled out their guns and began wildly firing at each other. When they were done, 28 people were hit by gunfire, including five children. One person died, but he was a bystander, not one of the armed persons in the gunfight.

I have seen thousands of people shooting military-style assault weapons in the forests over the last few years. Most were firing from the hip with the firearm held low and generally pointed at a target, using a stance you'd see in a Rambo poster, not aiming carefully. They were not holding the gun to the shoulder like most people would a hunting rifle and were not looking down the barrel through the sights or a scope. They assume that the extra fast-firing bullets will make up for any inaccuracy on their part. Americans do this because it is how they see them used in movies or TV. But no rifle is even remotely accurate when fired in this way.

The military and police rarely fire their weapons in fully automatic mode, but untrained people always do it. This is called "spray and pray." It never accomplishes what they want. Even firing a single round at a time can over-excite a shooter and throw his aim off. As a practical example, it is common for hunters with their first deer in their sights to freeze up and do nothing or fire wildly off-target; it's something called "Buck Fever." Their hearts are pounding, and they feel like they'll jump out of their chests. They begin to sweat and shake so they can hardly see straight. And this is to shoot their first deer, not a person! More importantly, deer do not have guns that they point and shoot back. If they did, few people would ever go hunting. An automatic weapon makes this much worse.

Part 5 of 5 – The Myths of Threats, Warning Shots, and Wounding Shots

It is essential to understand that if you are getting a gun for protection, you do not want to find out that you cannot fire it in self-defense until after you have pulled it out and pointed it at someone. I will offer solutions for additional training later in the chapter called "Advanced Training," but for now, here are some myths you must avoid.

First, do not plan on having a stand-off with a gun like you may have seen in movies. If I am in a situation as a *private citizen* where it becomes indispensable to kill an armed person with a gun, the last thing I want them to know is that I even have a firearm at all. Their first indication that I am armed with a firearm should come once they are fatally wounded and lying flat on the ground, dying because I have already shot them in the heart or lungs.

It would be best never to display your firearm to threaten someone. Do not display a gun until necessary and all other options are exhausted. If it is genuinely time to shoot someone, then a fatal decision should have already been made, and you do not want your opponent to know it is coming. Successful gunfights are not fair. There is no chivalry in them. Shooting and killing a person is not a sporting contest. After all other possible options are completely exhausted and there is nothing else left, it should be quick and lethal. But let me make one additional point completely clear:

Pointing a gun at someone is always the use of deadly force.

That is why it is a felony to do so without reasonable cause. A civilian's unjustifiably pointing a gun at someone is, in and of itself, the crime of assault. It is entirely different with police and military because official forces are already assumed to be armed and authorized to use force.

Second, you must never fire a warning shot. No police officer is either trained or allowed to do this. It is fiction reserved entirely for the movies.

Third, you should never shoot someone to try to wound them without killing them. No police officer is trained or allowed to do this, either. Trying either of these will only get you or some innocent person killed. They also allow your opponent to shoot and kill you while only disabled. The Lone Ranger always shot his foe in the shoulder to disarm him, shooting with a pistol from a great distance. That is a near impossibility, so please do not try to copy the Lone Ranger.

If you think otherwise, you should never own a firearm for self-defense. Doing so will only get you or some innocent person killed. Bluffing or playing around when you are not ready or able to commit to using a firearm to kill someone will seldom work.

These statements will be highly controversial with some folks. Some conservative and Republican conventional thinking is that you should pull out your gun whenever faced with intruders or potential threats to scare them away. Some will argue that guns can be used to bluff others into leaving or submitting. Gun sellers and right-wing media outlets love to propagate this foolish myth, but it is a huge mistake if you are not committed to killing that person when you draw and point your weapon. For every unprepared person who survives such an encounter, far more will end up dead.

Arguments for using firearms to warn or wound often come from highly publicized stories about an individual encounter where someone pulls out a gun, and the bad guy runs away. Usually, a woman in the story makes it even more dramatic. This makes you wonder what may have happened to her without pulling out the gun. Some even cite statistics about interviews with bad guys who say they do not want to attempt a crime against an armed home or person, but this makes no sense. A bad guy wouldn't know you had a gun unless you had a sign on your home that said, "Smith and Wesson protect this home." (I've seen such foolish welcome signs for burglars.) That creates more crime, not less. From my police experience, I know that guns are the third prominent item criminals want to steal from homes, only after large amounts of cash and illegal drugs like cocaine, heroin, and methamphetamine. Stealing other things are far down the list. Handguns and military assault-style weapons stolen from burglaries have a high street value and are easy to sell.

Some believe the first person to display a gun and fire will win a gunfight. But it isn't necessarily the first bullet fired that wins a gunfight. The first fatal shot does. If you are faced with a person armed with a gun, and they fire at you, they will often miss the first or first few shots. You will always want to use any available cover to protect yourself whenever possible. Some cover also allows you to take your time and fire the first fatal shot.

Yes, a gun can stop a crime, but only if the shooter is trained and capable of killing the offender. Informal and improper training will not work. Does this seem harsh, or is it something you are uncomfortable with? Good. You need to understand these things before getting a gun for protection. This is what using a gun to defend yourself will be like.

CHAPTER EIGHT

ADVANCED TRAINING

If you decide to train with a firearm, there are topics beyond safety to think about. The first step is easy: Orientation, safety, firing at targets, and cleaning a gun are not tricky. Some classes and instructors are good at this essential work, no matter where you live. Firearm safety and basic hunting classes are excellent places to meet interesting people who are there to help you, usually without a political agenda. Some courses are done outdoors, some at indoor ranges. Some states sponsor gun safety classes.

Once you have learned the basics of firing and maintaining your weapon, you may move on to practical uses in tactical situations. This is very different. Targets do not shoot back at you. If you need to shoot someone, he or she will not just hold still while you do it. You can experience mental and emotional processes that, if not adequately prepared for, make virtually everything you know about using a firearm worthless. The first time you must use a firearm in a tactical situation, you will not be ready if target shooting is all you have done.

When I started my police career in Washington State, all officers at the Basic Academy were sent to the Seattle Police Academy shooting range in South Seattle. The instructors were professionals, and the facility was well-run and safe. The officers could teach you to hit the target and handle your firearm safely. If you could not pass their standards during this training, you would flunk out of your career in police work. The class on shooting took just 40 hours.

Later, police departments realized that being able to hit a paper target had little to do with being able to handle a tactical situation. Under stress, that initial target training flew right out the window. Ongoing training was ordered, and competency was required to be renewed continuously with a new type of in-service training.

Those of us being retrained hated it at first because it was much work and made us sweat, but eventually, we began to see it as critically important. We had to exert ourselves at a range by running and shooting in the same exercise. We would do some shooting and then had to run until our pulses shot up, then stood or lay down and fired at the targets while our hearts were pounding. That replicated our responses to shooting situations. It required a great deal of discipline to be accurate while shooting, reloading quickly and then beginning to shoot again at multiple targets.

That is how you will feel when someone points a gun or is firing at you. Through training or experience, you can become more accustomed to it, and you may respond quite differently and be a bit calmer.

The next step in advanced training was addressing instant decision-making under extreme stress. Police departments were moving beyond primary weapons proficiency. It was not difficult to manually simulate the body's response to stress with heavy physical exertion, but this did not force other critical thinking functions to be tested. What evolved was called "Shoot, don't shoot" training. It was clever: Added to facing strict time limits and physical exertion to replicate stress, we had targets pop up unannounced. We would have no idea whether these instant "threats" were good or bad people. We couldn't just shoot any target that popped up. The target might represent a child running away from a kidnapper. Other targets posed lethal threats that justified our shooting them. Sometimes the line between shooting and not was thin. We had only a moment to make these decisions. Errors in judgment and thinking were not acceptable.

Then police training moved to its ultimate level to date. It was called "mock scenes." The trainers created an indoor location in Washington State called "Mock City." Trainees could go on "patrol" in this made-up city with realistic buildings and related props. It had academy staff as actors posing in situations the trainee did not know were coming. This replication of the real world, in which trainees had to face real-life and death situations and decisions, became excellent training.

The point of this training was for officers to feel like they were facing a genuine unannounced tactical threat. It wasn't just firearms training being tested; it also tested the mental functioning necessary to take a life or not. The real benefit lies in officers' thinking through scenarios in advance. That was well over half the battle. A trainee who could understand how to process and solve problems in realistic and stressful situations was well on the way to accessing that same critical thinking when it came time to use that skill on the job. Killing another person is difficult for any sane person to do. But this is a door to a place in the brain that, once found and opened, can be opened again when the need arises.

With shoot/don't shoot and mock situations, outcomes improved. The objective of preventing unnecessary police shootings was met with this training and quicker decision-making in deploying deadly force.

If you want to become proficient at defense with a firearm, you can find and attend similar training courses yourself, and you will understand what it will be like to fire at another person. You will either find this skill or possibly find that you can never do it. Either way, you will be a safer and more responsible gun owner. Your objective is to learn to beat people in combat without training or personal experience, and good instructors can address your questions and concerns.

I believe you don't get points for second place in a gunfight. If you are a gun owner, you need to be responsible, trained, and informed, or don't be one. We have far too many of the wrong kinds already.

CHAPTER NINE

SELF-ASSESSMENT – TAKE A SEAT ON THE COUCH

This may be the most crucial chapter in the book. How do you determine if you are an appropriate consumer to possess a gun or have one in your home for self-defense? Doing a proper self-risk assessment is a critical part of gun ownership. I wish many more Americans would ask that question before buying one. Because you live in America, this assessment is left up to you. Citizens in other countries have guns, but they get some help in this assessment. That is why other countries experience fewer gun problems per capita than Americans. Let's look at how this assessment works worldwide; then, you can see how you might want to proceed.

Most countries require an in-depth psychological assessment before allowing the possession of firearms. America does not. At most, some state laws prohibit licensing concealed weapons for people with histories of certain types of disqualifying mental illness that could lead to self-harm or harm to others.

There is a great story about buying guns in 16 other nations, by Audrey Carlsen and Sahil Chinoy, in the New York Times from March 2, 2018, and August 6, 2019, "How to Buy a Gun in Sixteen Countries." According to this review, the easiest country to get a gun was Yemen, where a firearm could be purchased online. That's it. In America, it is just a tiny bit more complicated. You must pass an instant background check for criminal convictions, domestic violence, and immigration status and wait for a three-day cooling-off period, at least when buying from a licensed dealer. Notoriously, "Gun Shows" have been lax in allowing anyone to walk in, buy a gun, and walk out with it, and private person-to-person sales aren't covered by laws at all.

By contrast, you must show that you are mentally stable enough to possess a gun in Japan, New Zealand, South Africa, Mexico, Australia, Austria, Canada, India, Germany, Britain, Brazil, Russia, Israel, and China. The test happens in various ways in different countries, but the idea is the same. A purchaser must be interviewed or pass a background check. Sometimes other people are interviewed about the buyer. Many people do not know they are mentally unstable, but their family and friends do!

Most countries also require the safe storage of firearms. Purchasers need a storage plan, and often, an inspection of the storage plan is required before the purchase.

Virtually all require a gun safety course. Purchasers must have basic ideas on using, firing, practicing with, or otherwise using a firearm before accidentally hurting or killing themselves or someone else. Brazil tests competence even further, requiring that the purchaser demonstrate hitting a target from 16 to 23 feet away at least 60 percent of the time. With a handgun, this is more difficult than a buyer might think and harder than it looks in a James Bond 007 movie.

Some countries ask why you want to buy a gun and what you plan to do with it. (Some potential buyers admit they want a gun to kill a specific person. Look up the story of Wendy Wein, who tried to hire a hitman to kill her husband.

Some people should never be allowed to buy a gun. Are you one of them? It is time to be honest. Test yourself in a few simple ways. First, do you use prescribed or OTC medications for mental or psychological issues of any type? Do the medications you take cause sleepiness, forgetfulness, or mood changes? Include anti-anxiety or anti-depressant medications and any other mood-altering drugs. Some medications have specific warnings for side effects, such as "Homicidal Rages." There is no shame here, but you must discuss it with your doctor or a qualified professional. If your doctor advises against it, reconsider getting a firearm. Your professional advisor might ask you to modify your plan to keep you and those around you safe. That may be easy to do. You might ask them if they have any reason to think you are a poor candidate to own a firearm.

The second question is: What do your family and friends think of your acquiring a firearm? If you are too unstable, they likely know this. You should carefully listen to them with an open mind. These discussions are an essential part of self-assessment before owning a firearm. We are not talking about mental illness here but about personality. Many people are clinically healthy but possess traits incompatible with safely owning a firearm, for instance, forgetfulness, clumsiness, or short temper. Your friends and family may love you but see these things clearly when you do not.

Bringing a firearm into a home for self-defense impacts everyone in the household. It should be a collective decision that every teenager and adult in the household understands. This will also facilitate making a proper safe storage plan. Other family members or housemates must know their responsibilities when a firearm is present. They must know and follow the rules.

Your self-assessment should be ongoing. Mental states can change, as can relationships. If depression sets in, that's a reason to secure a weapon more carefully. Loss of a loved one, loss of a job, or loss of money can trigger significant changes in a person's mental state. Another red flag is a relationship showing signs of deterioration, where behavior becomes controlling. Keep an open mind to these types of changes in yourself or others.

America's suicide rate explains why prospective gun owners need a psychological assessment before considering gun ownership. A man with a gun in the house is eight times more likely to commit suicide, according to a Stanford study published in June 2020. A Harvard study in 2010 indicated that of 38,664 suicides in America, 19,392 were suicides by firearm. The number of others killed by firearms in the same period was 11,078. That is almost twice as many people intentionally kill themselves using a gun in their homes than those who are shot otherwise. If a person attempts self-harm with a firearm, he or she will be successful 85% of the time. With drugs, that rate is only 3%.

Suicide is impactful, not just to persons who kill themselves, but to their families, friends, neighbors, and aid workers. You may not like what I am about to tell you now, but you need to understand it. Suicides are not like TV, movies, or video games. They are unfathomably gruesome. Most close-range firearm suicides result in large parts of the head being blown off. Sometimes just the bottom jaw is left, with the upper skull and brains blown apart into a mist that covers everything in the room. It is a mess. It looks like the walls were painted with blood, brains, and tiny pieces of skull. This is always the result when a high-powered rifle or shotgun is used.

When people use firearms to kill themselves, someone else must discover and clean up the mess. This happens 55 times daily in America, 365 days a year, especially on holidays like Thanksgiving and Christmas.

The length of a rifle or shotgun makes it harder to use for suicide. Handguns are much more dangerous in these cases. People killing themselves with a rifle or shotgun must place it under their jaw or mouth, often using their toes to fire it. It is not easy to do. Handguns can make direct contact with the head or chest to shoot it efficiently. All firearms must be kept in a way to minimize risks of suicide, but the risk is far greater with a handgun.

Many states now have laws called Extreme Risk Protection Orders for removing firearms from a person who is a threat to themselves or others, even if they have not yet committed a crime. Don't wait for that.

Many drunks or alcoholics either do not know or do not admit that they have this condition. Alcoholism is a significant reason not to get a firearm. Alcohol and firearms cannot be mixed.

When I was a detective on a specialized team some years ago, we were all very close and liked to have a drink some evenings after work. When we did, we all locked up our weapons in a secure area and double-checked for guns before someone had as much as a sip of beer. If you cannot accept this concept as an absolute requirement or have a drinker in your house who might have access to the firearm when intoxicated, you should never buy, own, or allow a firearm in your home.

The following risk factor around having a firearm in the house is relationships. You should not have a gun if you have struck another person in your household or broken any of that person's property in anger. If a person in your household has struck you or broken your property, you should not allow a gun to be present if that person has access. Statistically speaking, people who strike or break the property of others in domestic situations will often be willing to use a gun if one is available, especially if drunk and angry.

Even in America, where our gun laws are lax, domestic violence can disqualify a person from gun ownership; however, often, domestic violence gets discovered only if a person is convicted.

Asking these questions is part of your self-assessment of whether you should have a gun in your house. Your self-assessment needs to be brutally honest and forthright. You don't need to tell anyone or overly dwell on the past, but you must face the realities of the impacts of not considering these matters before buying a gun. Lay these things on the table and give them careful consideration.

Further, assuming your household is safe, do you also have a plan, the time, money, and facilities to properly learn how to possess and use a firearm for home self-defense? Currently, .357 ammunition for S&W Model 66 handguns costs around $.70 to a little over $1.00 per round of ammunition. An average training session will use roughly 250 rounds, costing up to $250, to get much of anything done on a training course. You will need dozens of these sessions to attain a high level of proficiency. Ongoing training will cost hundreds more. Allow four to five times as much training if you plan to use an automatic weapon. Ammunition will cost more than the gun itself. Tactical ammunition will cost far more than these training target rounds. But if you cannot provide adequate training, you will be useless with the gun in home defense.

Where are you going to get experience? Unless you live in rural Montana or Alaska, you probably can't just walk out the back door and set up a shooting range. There are many commercial ranges in most parts of the country, indoors and outdoors, and many have excellent instructors who can help you get started, but again, you must assess these costs before buying a firearm. Many ranges will not allow military assault-style semi-automatic weapons on their premises. Very few allow fully automatic weapons to be fired. Have you considered these facts?

A final question for your self-assessment is whether you are dedicated enough to follow through. You can be lazy about many activities in your life, but not this one. A firearm is not for you if you get bored and taper off on projects. It would be best to treat a firearm as ultimately deadly 100% of the time, 24 hours a day, 365 days a year. Having one for general home defense is an endeavor that requires a commitment to make and follow through.

Guns in the hands of responsible owners might make them, their homes, and their other family members safer, but only if done correctly.

CHAPTER TEN

NEGLIGENCE & THE VERY END OF YOUR LIFE

In South Carolina, on Christmas day in December of 2021, at 2:30 in the afternoon, the Henderson County Sheriff's Office responded to a terrible and utterly preventable call for help. When emergency workers arrived, they found a 3-year-old girl had suffered a gunshot wound. She had accessed an unsecured firearm and shot herself but still clung to life. This is one of the worst calls any police officer or medic can respond to. No matter how experienced or battle-hardened someone is, this is one of the calls that rips your heart.

Due to the devastating injuries, the child was airlifted to nearby Mission Hospital and underwent surgery. The heroic aid workers and doctors did everything possible to save her life. Medical staff is also profoundly impacted by these senseless injuries to small children. After over 72 agonizing hours for this shocked community, police officers, medical workers, and family, the small child died of her terrible wounds. This will be a Christmas to remember for everyone involved but in the most devastating way possible.

Although this has been covered in other chapters, I want to emphasize it again. It's that important. Like alcohol and guns are a toxic match, so are kids and guns. Before buying, training with, transporting, or owning a gun, you must comprehensively assess this issue. If a child gets their hands on your gun, something virtually unimaginable up to this point in your life will possibly happen. Your life will never be the same again. You can forget all your dreams and plans or any semblance of everyday life after that time. You will think of it every minute of every day until you die. It is an image that will never leave your mind. This will be a life-ending event that could happen to you.

Besides the horror you would feel, you could also have significant liability, criminal in many states, and civil liability in any state if you did not secure your firearm and it was used to harm someone else.

Improperly stored or mishandled firearms are responsible for killing or wounding 18,000 kids from 1 to 19 years old in America each year. Guns are the leading cause of death for this age group. Of that above number, over 5,100 are aged 17 and younger, so it isn't just young adults. There do not need to be any such incidents or accidents.

Although you cannot control what others do, you can ensure you will not be a part of this problem or statistic. If you decide to get a firearm, you must review all the safety advice you have read in this book. Make a list and think it over. Use it as a checklist. It is not all that difficult, but you must have a safety plan and keep to it.

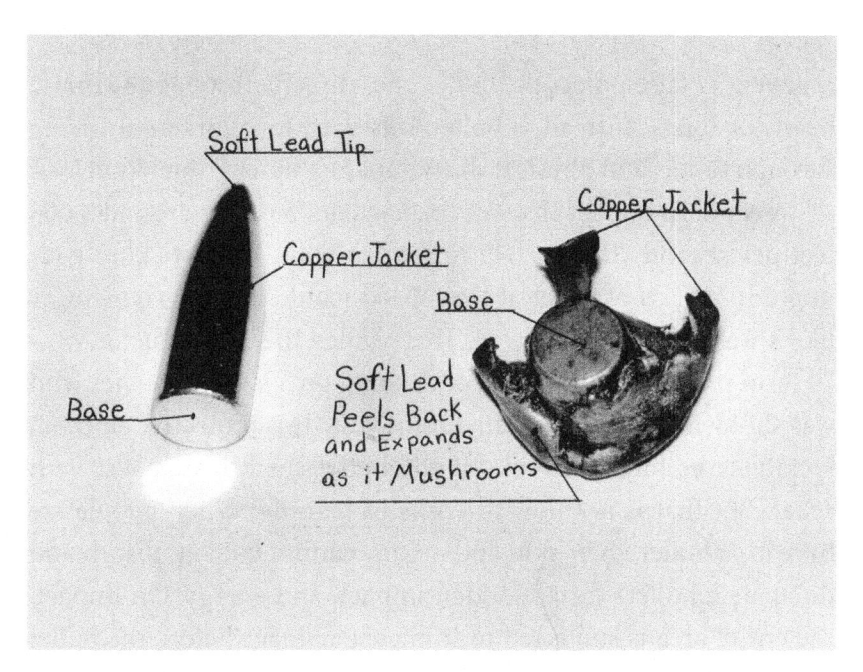

A typical unfired non-military round to the left, along side of one on the right, after firing and penetrating tissue and bone with full expansion.

CHAPTER ELEVEN

~

HOW A BULLET KILLS

Although it is easy to understand how a gun fires, very few people understand how a bullet works after it leaves the barrel of a firearm and strikes its target. Most people think a bullet kills someone or an animal because it punches a hole in them. This is generally false unless the bullet goes directly through the brain, heart, or lungs. Instead, a bullet kills with force, internal slicing through tissue, and physical shock, not just shock from blood loss.

A modern bullet can leave the barrel of a rifle at around 3,000 feet per second. That's 2,045 miles per hour. Even sticking your finger in a glass of water at that speed would destroy your finger like it was hitting a brick wall. That's called the "shock factor."

You probably have seen a policeman on TV or in movies who was shot while wearing a bulletproof vest. This protective clothing luckily saves him. He looks at the bullet stuck in the vest with relief. But that is not how it works in real life. When people are hit with a bullet, their skin and organs cannot quickly absorb and dissipate a bullet's force, sudden impact, and energy. On impact, the entire area is subjected to immense damage before the bullet enters. Sometimes this is fatal in and of itself. The shock can be so great with some ammunition that parts of a person's body seem to vaporize. In slow motion, this looks like a mist dissipating into the air. Even with less impact, a bullet hitting a bulletproof vest hits the officer at such a high speed that it knocks out his or her breath. The vest and outer clothing can be pushed deep into the chest, even though the bullet has not penetrated anything.

So many officers with "bulletproof" vests were being killed in the early days of their use that a metal "shock plate" was added to the front of the vest over the heart and lungs. That helped spread the force of a bullet over a larger area, making it less destructive. Today many vests have ceramic shock plates that shatter with the first bullet strike. That absorbs the shock, like the crumple zones in a modern car. Bulletproof vests save many officers, but those officers can still suffer significant injuries because of the shock and energy of a bullet hitting them.

Most non-military tactical bullets have lead tips, and some are open at the end. They are called "hollow-point" bullets. As soon as they hit something water-based, like an animal or a body, the relatively soft tip flattens out and begins to "mushroom," growing more extensive than the original bullet diameter. As it flattens out on the end and opens, pieces begin to shear off and spin into the surrounding tissue and organs. A single bullet at high speed can deposit hundreds of pieces of shrapnel into the body. That is why some victims of gunshots have multiple surgeries to remove bullet "fragments." Some will have stray bullet parts in their bodies that show up on X-rays for the rest of their lives.

Hollowpoint bullets can deform more than solid bullets. Hollowpoints can also have small scoring on the copper jacket near the bullet tip. This causes the copper part of the bullet to open further, and the expanding copper pieces, or "claws," rip through an even larger area just like a buzz saw. The damage from this type of bullet goes far beyond the area of the bullet's original diameter. This expanding and fragmenting of the bullet are designed to hit as many veins and arteries as possible on the way in before stopping. Expansion and damage from the slicing copper pieces and energy shock are intended. Most victims of a gunshot who die do so from the tissue damage in the surrounding area and the catastrophic bleeding that is associated with it.

Bullets not fully encased in metal jackets over the lead tips are sometimes called "dum-dums," although this term is not used much anymore. It was used extensively during WWI and began to fall out of use in the 1960s. Still, this language used in the Geneva Conventions describes a general category of bullets that expand after hitting someone.

Bluntnose, full metal jackets, and slower and cheap ammunition also have purposes. They are used for target practice and military use. They cost only a fraction of the cost of tactical rounds like the ones that police officers have in their duty weapons. Bullets designed for target practice do not work well in killing someone because of their low velocity, small size, and low kinetic energy. Still, many people use these bullets in their guns for self-defense because they do not understand the ballistics of bullets and the difference between the two uses.

Many inexpensive target rounds do not have copper jackets, and this is to save costs. They are just a lump of lead. The shells are thin and often made of less expensive metals or plastic. They have less powder, are designed only to shoot paper targets at a range, and cannot contain the pressures of exploding high-velocity tactical rounds used for self-defense or police work.

Besides the damage caused by the shock and force of a bullet, there are secondary injuries from bullet wounds that can also have lasting impacts on a shot person. I was working early one morning in my police career when I was called to a shooting at a Radio Shack store. When we got there, a guy was lying on the ground. He and the store were a bloody mess, but he was alive. I was a detective then and was sent to the hospital with this victim to recover the bullets from his body to hold as evidence. We went to Harborview Hospital, a top-level trauma facility with some of the best surgeons in the world. I was invited in by the surgical team, put on a gown and mask, and stood by the guy's head so I was not in the way. This way, doctors could hand me the bullets, and I could see where they came from and testify about it. This could spare the surgeons from coming to court later to testify at a trial.

I find surgery fascinating, but it is not for everyone to see in person. Emergency room surgical processes are not gentle. Time is everything when it comes to saving a person's life. The doctors quickly took a saw, like a skill saw you might have at home, and sawed his chest open in just a few moments. Then they stuck in massive clamps that pulled his chest open from the sides. One of the bullets that didn't go through and into the chamber had struck his heart. They pulled his heart from his chest cavity and stitched up the small tear on the side while it was still beating. This was super cool to watch in person. They reached into his chest cavity and pulled out a big hand full of coagulated blood. Watching this was less enjoyable. After they took out the blood, they pulled out two bullets, one from his lung cavity and one lodged into his liver. The surgeons gave me the bullets, and I stuck them into a paper evidence bag in some cloth so the blood on them would dry out and not rot.

These shots had been fired while the suspect and victim were fighting. They entered from the top of the victim's shoulders and went through his chest cavity in a big X shape, crossing in about the middle of his chest. They were the result of a gun attack that had gone very wrong. The first shot had hit him in the leg (not unusual for a small automatic handgun which is notoriously inaccurate in combat stress), and then he had fought with the attacker hand-to-hand. The attacker finally delivered the second and third shots at point-blank range, pointing down from the top of his shoulders while they were both on the ground wrestling. Any more powerful weapon or proper bullets would have killed him almost instantly.

The victim didn't die, but even though he lived, his mind was destroyed by the lack of oxygen for so long due to his excessive internal bleeding. When he woke up in the hospital, he asked me who I was. I told him I was Detective Hurst. Then he asked where he was. I said he was in the hospital. He asked why. I said he was shot. He responded, "I'm shot? Who are you?" And we would begin the same series of questions repeatedly. This 20-second loop is all his mind could contain, and it never stopped being like that, first for weeks, then for months. We eventually figured out that his wife's ex-boyfriend attempted this murder to get her back.

The point here is that bullets can destroy a person's life and the lives of those around them in many ways. It also shows how a handgun can fire a bullet that does not do what bullets on TV or in the movies do.

The bad guy, in this case, got a "gun" and did not know much about it or the bullets it contained. It was just a gun, like any other, and he thought the bullets would accomplish what he wanted. He planned to walk in, shoot the gun at the guy, hit him in the heart, see him fall dead on the floor, and that would be the end of it. Then he would get his old girlfriend back. Instead, this first shot with his semi-automatic handgun hit the victim in the leg. When he finally made what might have been fatal shots, the bullets failed to do what he wanted them to because they were small, slow target rounds. This bad guy's knowledge of guns and bullets was average for most people in America today. This may surprise you, but it is true.

A Myth & Military Ammunition

Police bullets and military bullets are different and have vastly different purposes. Police and hunting bullets are designed to kill people or animals. By contrast, military bullets sometimes kill but are designed more for wounding and not killing or injuring people as seriously as nonmilitary and police bullets. There is a simple reason for this. Bullets like the ones that the police use and those used for killing a deer are illegal in military conflicts. They have been illegal since 1899, and their use is an international war crime today. Although people who love their military-style weapons and believe that they are the ultimate killing machines do not believe this, here is the actual language from the Geneva Conventions that makes them illegal:

> *The Contracting Parties agree to abstain from the use of bullets which expand or flatten easily in the human body, such as*

bullets with a hard envelope which does not entirely cover the core or is pierced with incisions." Declaration (IV,3) concerning Expanding Bullets. The Hague, 29 July 1899.

According to Section 6(1)(b)(xix), "[e]mploying bullets which expand or flatten easily in the human body, such as bullets with a hard envelope which does not entirely cover the core or is pierced with incisions", constitutes a war crime in international armed conflicts.

Many will vehemently deny that this exists, and some will point out that America has not signed onto some of the more recent elements of the Geneva Conventions. The second point is valid, but the provisions about bullets from 1899 still apply, and the U.S. did sign these. Moreover, consider how America treats expanding bullets in its established rules for armed service members in combat. Here are but a few examples:

United States of America
The US Military Field Manual (1956) states: "Usage, has ... established the illegality of ... the scoring of the surface or the filing off of the ends of the hard cases of bullets

United States of America
The US Air Force Pamphlet (1976) states: International law has condemned dum dum ... bullets because of types of injuries and inevitability of death. Usage and practice has also determined that it is per se illegal ... to use irregularly shaped bullets or to score the surface or to file off the end of the hard cases of the bullets which cause them to expand upon contact and thus aggravate the wound they cause.

United States of America
The US Instructor's Guide (1985) stresses the prohibition of "irregular-shaped bullets such as dum-dum bullets The Guide also provides: "In addition to the grave breaches of the Geneva Conventions, the following acts are further examples of war crimes: using ... forbidden arms or ammunition such as dum-dum bullets.

You can see from these quotations that America's military field manuals prohibit dum-dums, which is just another term for expanding bullets. People will argue vociferously against the idea that military ammunition is less deadly than civilian and police ammunition. Online, you can see thousands of pages of posts calling this statement liberal nonsense, a myth. But they believe that is a myth. Let's look at the facts.

Military bullets are commonly called "full metal jacket" bullets. The inside is made of lead or, in some cases, steel. The "jacket" is a copper cover that goes from one end of the bullet to the other. It looks like a little copper missile from the blunt end to the point. It is not made of soft lead on the tip. The tip is not flat. The tip does not have a hole in it. The copper shroud does not have any scoring along its side. Those features would make the bullet expand and spin off pieces into the person being shot and do more damage. Military bullets will not deform much upon entering the body. They remain the same size as they go through a body instead of growing three, four, or even five times larger as it travels through human tissue. Expanding bullets would do almost infinitely more damage, and the military rarely uses them except in controlled and permitted circumstances.

Police do not want to use a firearm until necessary, but when they do, they mean for it to kill and not merely wound a person. The military realized that wounding people requires soldiers to attend to a wounded comrade, thus tying up the fighting force in assisting people who need medical attention. Advocates will also attack this statement for military bullets. They do not understand the goal of most warfare. They think wars are glorious events about the macho killing of others. The actual goal of war is for one side to prevail, making one's opponents an ineffective fighting force until it surrenders, ending the conflict as quickly as possible. If that objective can be achieved with fewer deaths in modern warfare, so much the better.

Bullet Performance & Uses

The old movies of police firing warning shots or shooting to wound but not kill are complete fiction. No police officer has ever had any such training. When necessary to shoot, police fire only to kill, aiming at "center body mass," or the area in roughly the middle of a person's chest, where the heart and lungs are located. Hitting a person's lungs or heart will usually cause catastrophic internal bleeding, sometimes killing the person in a few seconds and usually within a few minutes. Plummeting blood pressure will cause unconsciousness, and death follows. Just wounding does not neutralize a threat. Police do not aim for the shoulder, head, or stomach areas. A person's head is too small a target.

 The ammunition used affects how well a handgun serves its police tactical or home defense purpose. The .357 magnum round for a revolver and the .40 caliber Smith & Wesson automatic round are excellent bullets for self-defense. They are large and powerful enough to stop someone. Small-caliber ammunition, like a .22, or small-caliber handgun rounds like a .25 or a .32, can be deadly but often are not. Many of them shoot low-velocity bullets. A .22 pistol shoots a bullet at roughly 1,200 feet per second, and the bullet is very light. These weapons are unsuitable for self-defense because they can't reliably kill someone.

When I worked in Tukwila, Washington, a close friend, a fellow former law enforcement officer, and colleague responded to an active shooter in a large shopping mall. He saw the bad guy with the gun and ran up to save others. The bad guy shot him seven times with a .22 caliber rifle before my friend took the gun away. Although some gunshot wounds gave him difficulties for years, none were fatal. None stopped him at the time, nor did they keep him from disarming the shooter.

Smaller handguns and rounds are foolish for self-defense because they will not stop a bad guy. And no, the Walther PPK that James Bond carries is not what you are looking for.

Many small-caliber handguns women buy and carry for self-defense are nowhere near adequate to stop an attacker. It is a mistake to rely on them because they can easily be taken away and used against the owner, even by someone who has already been shot with it! Some will say that a woman can't shoot a .357 magnum revolver or a .40 caliber Smith & Wesson automatic handgun due to the recoil. I disagree as this is more about proper training than the gun and bullet itself. I also think using the proper firearm and bullet is necessary, or not using one at all is better.

A friend recently told me the story of a woman from Alaska who goes running in bear country with a small .22 handgun. People always tell her that she cannot kill a grizzly bear with a .22, to which she responds, "Of course. I know that. If a bear attacks, the bullet is for me!" This woman has a keen awareness of bullet performance.

Different firearms can fire a variety of different size bullets, projectiles, or shells. A .22 is a small caliber bullet; on the other end of the spectrum, one of the largest bullets is a .50 caliber. A .50 caliber can kill a person almost two miles away. They were used in fighter airplanes to shoot through the sides of Navy Destroyer ships in WWII to sink them. But even the best gun, without the proper ammunition and understanding of how it works and where to place the bullet, can render it useless in a tactical encounter.

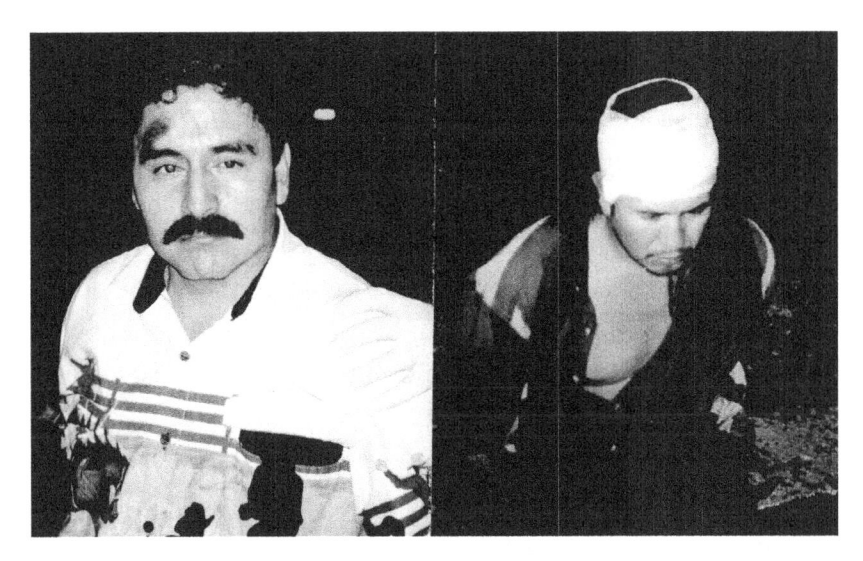

"Little Cowboy" and his partner tried to kill my partner with a pearl handeled .45 automatic during a bust. It was a close combat handgun fight with no shots fired.

CHAPTER TWELVE

HOME DEFENSE ALTERNATIVES

There are many options for home defense, ranging from cheap to expensive. They may serve your needs better than procuring a firearm. Below, we discuss alternatives to keeping a gun in your house.

GUN GUIDE FOR DEMOCRATS

Part 1 of 5 - Baseball

If you want a gun to defend yourself in your home, you may have missed an alternative so common that you may never have thought of it. It is something your kids, or you, probably used at some time in your life. It's a baseball bat. I know it's not sexy like a brand-new automatic military-style assault AR-15 with 30-round clips, but guess what? It often can beat a gun in close combat. If your intruder is not armed, an aluminum or wood baseball will beat them every time.

Baseball bats are cheap, super available, and pose little to no risk if you store a few in your home. Keep one by the door and one by the couch where you watch TV. No one will even pay much attention. It just looks like you didn't clean up your house very well.

There is one other huge benefit of a baseball bat over a handgun. Unlike a firearm, it is, quite literally, the worst tool in your house to use to kill yourself. Suicide by baseball bat is very uncommon.

Part 2 of 5 – Grizzly Bears

Not interested in the concept of hitting someone with a baseball bat? Another product that can be very effective at stopping an intruder, even one with a gun, is bear spray. It is highly effective at stopping a charging Grizzly bear. It is not just the tiny self-protection personal spray the size of lipstick you may have seen, but the larger product that hikers carry when giant bears are present, like on Glacier National Park back-country hikes.

One of the most popular brands is Counter Assault, which comes in 10-ounce spray cans and can reach 40 feet to stop a Grizzly. Your bedroom is perhaps 20' across. This product can be purchased for around $60. It comes in a pouch that you can wear on your belt when hiking in bear country or fits on your bedside table.

The website for Counter Assault claims that it will stop charging Grizzly bears 92% of the time. From personal experience with this product, I can tell you its effects will be much stronger on people than on bears. This may stop a person without using deadly force.

There are several benefits to having a spray in your home for self-defense. You are within range to use it anywhere in a common-sized house. You do not need to be very accurate. Anything in front of you will be inundated. An invader will likely be on their knees within a second, screaming and convulsing violently or trying to leave the area.

The spray continues for eight seconds. You can give multiple short doses or empty the can all at once. Strong effects last 15 to 45 minutes. Milder effects last about two hours. If you do not get it in your eyes or breathe it in yourself, you have more than enough time to call the police, tie up your assailant with restraints, or just run away.

You could restrain an intruder with handcuffs, but not with personal or fantasy ones like people have for other reasons. They are not the right product because they can easily break or be opened. If you want handcuffs, ensure they are of good quality, like the ones the police use, and learn to use them properly.

Although I cannot say for sure, I suspect it would be challenging to commit suicide with this product, should anybody want to try it. If bad guys steal it in a burglary, they will probably use it on their friends when drunk at a party to see what it does. It will never be seen as a cool weapon. Losing one from theft is far less severe than losing a gun.

That all being said, this product is not entirely non-lethal. Although extremely rare, there have been deaths from its use. This usually happens when people have restricted breathing from the products or pre-existing medical conditions. It is not a product to be used without necessity, but in my opinion, a person entering your home and attacking you more than justifies its use.

Once deployed, pepper spray will linger, quickly affecting you and the intruder. You must leave and wait for the police outdoors unless you also access a gas mask. Protesters often use them, and you can find them for sale on the Internet.

Before having or using bear spray, I would also check with all local, state, and federal laws, depending on where you live. This product is considered a firearm in Canada and is not legal without the same permitting process as a gun. Never take or keep it somewhere it might not be legal, like courthouses or airports where weapons are not permitted. The bear spray must also be kept out of the reach of children.

Part 3 of 5 – Electrical Solutions
Another option to consider for self-defense is an electrical device to disable an attacker. You might be familiar with the product called a "Taser" that many police carry.

I must tell you that I have a bit of a personal bias regarding electricity—it frightens me. When I was a 2-year-old, I was sitting on a concrete floor and stuck a pin into a wall socket. It is the only early childhood memory I can recall, but I can still see it as if it were just a moment ago. Then, a few years ago, I was hiking in the mountains when heavy rain and a terrible thunderstorm overcame me. A shaft of lightning hit 10 feet in front of me. The lightning knocked me back and shocked the heck out of me. That only reinforced my misgivings about electricity. It's excruciating. I'm sensitive to being confronted by electricity.

A Taser will work well in stopping most people, at least for a few moments, or even a minute, but just until you get them under control, or you can run away. A Taser fires two darts that stick into the target's body. They are like tiny hypodermic needles with hooks on the ends. They are attached to long electrical wires that carry the charge into the body. The charge is both painful and, in most people, temporarily disabling. Although a person will recover quickly from the shock, nobody wants it to happen again.

There are other electrical defense devices as well. Some work on contact. A few are designed for people, and some are specifically designed to use on cattle. You have likely heard of a "cattle prod." It is just a very powerful direct-contact cow Taser. Some devices have two electrodes separated by a couple of inches. When you push a button, a large arc of electricity jumps across these electrodes, making a frightening electrical crackling sound. As someone who stuck a pin in a wall socket and got hit by lightning, it has significantly impacted me!

Prods for use on people are called "stun guns" and are widely available on the internet for between $10 and $400. If you click one on, they look terrifying, and many people are scared away. That may be their best use, although I am not recommending it. If it fails in a tactical situation, I can guarantee that a bad guy will use it on you, even if to see what it does to a person. Again, I oppose displaying weapons you are unwilling, able, and trained to use.

Police officers trained with and carrying Tasers are required to have been shocked by one. There is a good reason for this. They need to know what it does. If you carry a stun gun, you should consider the same thing, but you will not like it.

Part 4 of 5 – Physical Training & Home Defense

Many people take physical self-defense or martial arts courses taught by professionals. Some of these are excellent and have the added benefit of getting students into shape. You would be surprised at how some physical training and a self-defense course can help protect yourself if you are ever attacked or threatened by someone. Most bad guys try to prey on defenseless people who do not fight back. Even some simple skills and voice commands can empower you to make an attacking person quickly retreat. These types of courses are easy to find anywhere in the United States. They can also be a healthy and fun place to meet other people with similar objectives. People with some skills they have practiced have more confidence if faced with a threat. An attacker will sense this quickly and often move on while you call the police or retreat yourself.

Part 5 of 5 - Never Bring a Gun to a Knife Fight
I like movies. Movies are a universal language that illuminates ideas and concepts we can all relate to. Of course, movies are also mostly nonsense. But we enjoy the suspension of disbelief for two hours. People know they can't put on a mask and a cape and then fly; however, they'll rely on movies to get most of their beliefs about guns. You have probably seen a movie where a bad guy pulls out a knife or sword and does some fancy hand movements when facing the good guy. The good guy pulls out a handgun and shoots from 100 feet away. The bad guy with the knife or sword falls dead on the ground with a single shot. The people in the scene and the movie theater are impressed, and the audience howls with laughter. It works great for Paul Neuman and Harrison Ford every time. It makes sense, right? Not so much.

In truth, if two people are at least 20 feet apart, where one determined person has a knife and the other has a handgun, the person with the knife will win the encounter roughly nine times out of ten against most people with a handgun. "Win" is an interesting term here as it means that the person with the knife will inflict a fatal wound before being shot or injured by the person with the handgun, and that is if they were even shot at all. A knife is often better than a handgun at around 20 feet away or less. There are multiple reasons for this.

Most police shootings occur within six feet of their target. Police can't often shoot and hit people with a handgun from more than six feet away. Civilians will find it even more difficult than officers do for three reasons. First, handguns are not highly accurate beyond 10 to 20 feet. Aiming a gun, holding it steady, slowly exhaling, squeezing the trigger carefully, and hitting much of anything beyond a short distance takes time. Unlike what you have seen in hundreds of movies, a quick draw would rarely hit a target 50 feet away, absent hundreds of hours of practice. Second, the knife will win the fight because if you are attacked and are not properly trained, massive amounts of adrenaline will course through your veins, causing your heart to pound so hard you can hardly see straight. You can't aim well in that condition. Don't count on your handgun being very effective beyond six feet most of the time.

Third, another problem with shooting in a knife attack is that most of the guns people buy for protection, especially women, have very short barrels, so they are concealable or lightweight. The shorter the gun barrel, the less accurate it will be. You aim a gun by lining up the front sight with the rear sight while pointing it at the middle of your target. A gun finds its accuracy based on the rear and front sight distance. Shorten that distance; you can't hit much beyond six feet in a gunfight. In the meantime, the bad guy can cross the room, grab your weapon, and stab you.

James Bond may carry a Walther PPK with its short barrel, but given a sock with a rock in it, you might beat 007 in an armed encounter and never get shot. These very short, small-caliber handguns are notoriously inaccurate and seriously underpowered.

One of my favorite movie scenes is from the Mel Brooks comedy Blazing Saddles, where a Gene Wilder character, the Waco Kid, shoots and hits some dynamite from about three miles away with his handgun, blowing up the town. This is a joke for the audience to laugh at, but most movies are not comedies like this one. They make these types of shots or unrealistic firearm performances seem real.

I once worked with a sheriff's deputy earlier in my career, Detective Michael Raburn, who went to serve a court order in Seattle on March 27, 1984. The resident at the location opened the door and stabbed Detective Raburn in the chest with a WWII sword. Detective Raburn fired several shots as he fell back while retreating, but he died shortly afterward. What is accurate about a knife instead of a gun encounter is even more accurate when a sword is involved. A sword, especially in the hands of a person with some training, is almost infinitely more dangerous than a firearm.

After being hit numerous times by bullets, I have seen people returning fire. A book called *Street Survival - Tactics for Armed Encounters,* by Special Agent Ronald J. Adams and Lieutenant Thomas M. McTernan and Charles Remsberg, popular in the 1980s, has an example of a police firefight where a man who was hit 33 times by police firing 9mm handguns, was still shooting back. No such thing happens when a major injury is inflicted with a sword.

I am not suggesting that police carry samurai swords, but for home defense, you should know that a long sharp kitchen knife in the hands of the right person is a more dangerous weapon than a gun at very close ranges.

Many police officers who were shot and killed in the line of duty (as opposed to suicides) over the years were killed with their service weapons. In Washington State some years ago, three consecutive police officers killed in the line of duty were killed with their own handguns. Although most officers fire their weapons within six feet, using a handgun at such close range poses the problem of someone taking the gun away. Try grabbing a sword or even a 12-inch kitchen knife out of someone's hand. It's virtually impossible to do without getting a severe or fatal injury.

Once, I was serving a narcotics search warrant in the Seattle area. The suspect in the case was a bad guy whom I had sent to prison twice in the previous decade. He opened his front door after we announced that we had a warrant. Out came his hand with a gun. It was a close call, but I grabbed the gun before he could fire it at me. My finger ended up behind the hammer, and I pushed the gun barrel into the air as I squashed the door against him to crush his arm. I got him to let go of the gun, and after a short scuffle, he was arrested. If he had been armed with a sword, I would have likely been killed at such a close range.

A sharp weapon can go through many ballistic vests. Ballistic vests are layers of fiber designed to absorb the shock and impact from spinning bullets, not sharp-cutting-edged weapons. Even highly trained police officers wearing vests can get stabbed.

At closer ranges, within six feet, keeping control of one's firearm gets more complicated. One night, I was assigned to a federal narcotics task force. My partner was doing an undercover buy of a large amount of cocaine from a member of the Sinaloa Cowboys, a highly violent Mexican organized crime family. We recognized them well from a distance because many carried pearl-handled .45 automatic handguns and had Brahma bull stickers on their truck windows and lariats on their rearview mirrors. They also wore gold necklaces depicting the patron saint of drug traffickers, Jesus Malverde (not recognized by the Catholic Church, I might add). We thought it was an excellent "uniform" for an organized crime family, but we remembered they were also exceptionally violent and thought nothing of killing others.

As the bust went down, my partner Frank was wearing a wire so we could hear what was happening, but only one of us on the bust team spoke Spanish. Frank was fluent and spoke in Spanish with a bad guy known on the street as "Little Cowboy." But with the language issue, there was some confusion with the bust signal, and things began to go wrong.

Little Cowboy pulled out his .45 automatic and tried to shoot Frank in the abdomen as they sat side by side in the truck's cab. Frank grabbed the gun and pushed Little Cowboy's hand up, so the gun was pointed at the top of the truck. Frank pulled out his handgun and tried to shoot Little Cowboy in the mid-section near his heart and lungs, which would quickly be fatal. Little Cowboy grabbed Frank's gun and pushed it up too, and as their struggle went on, our team arrived and jerked open the door. By then, Frank had used the butt of his gun to pound a significant dent in Little Cowboy's head. When we opened the door, both men fell out, dropped their guns in the dark on the side of the road, and continued wrestling. A second bad guy hiding nearby showed up and had to be restrained as well.

By then, we were all scrambling in the dark with guns, gravel, blood, and bodies everywhere. We got things sorted out without anyone being shot or killed. No shots were ever fired. The point is that even with highly trained and experienced police detectives, guns can get grabbed. If either had pulled out a knife, the outcome would likely have been fatal for one or both. In a movie, you will never see anything like this, but you might in real life.

Cash, drugs, and firearms are what people are looking for in most home invasion robberies. Pictured here is $438,000 in cash, cocaine and an automatic assault-style weapon.

CHAPTER THIRTEEN

HOME INVASION ROBBERIES

It's time to cover probably the scariest firearm encounter that most people in America fear today:

HOME INVASION ROBBERIES!

They are scary. Every time one happens, it makes front-page news. Right-wing media outlets tell you they happen all the time. They want to terrify you. They detail the horror of someone breaking in, tying you up, and you and your family being tortured, raped, robbed, and killed. These media outlets and some far-right politicians want you to think about this because it keeps viewers glued to their stations. Besides attracting advertising revenue, this fearmongering delivers donations to their favorite political candidates and votes to right-wing politicians.

To clarify, a "burglary" is an entry and theft done secretly in a residence or certain buildings, which is typical. A "robbery" is a person-to-person confrontation. Done in private residences, robberies are uncommon. Many home burglaries (or even home robberies) could have been prevented by a sound home security system that deters, detects, and scares criminals away.

In many home invasion robberies, the victim knows the intruder, and the invaders are there for a known reason or relationship. You will never hear this on FOX News. Let me explain:

I once arrested a man named Troy Marlowe for drug trafficking. He agreed, as many people do, to cooperate as a witness against his higher-level suppliers. Our objective was always to get as far up the distribution chain as possible and file cases against those who run criminal enterprises, not just the lower-level workers. During his cooperation, I became aware of claims from others that Marlowe also ran a side business doing armed home invasion robberies.

I asked him about this, and he said it was a very lucrative business. He knew his victims would never testify against him because they were criminals. He told me in detail about how he and his crew, dressed in all-black outfits with face coverings like Ninja warriors, moved quickly, broke into houses, drew guns, and tied everyone up at gunpoint. He robbed them of cash and drugs. Competitors in the drug business do that to each other all the time. It has probably happened somewhere in America since you began reading this story. It's what criminals do. These are seldom reported to the police, and the criminals know it.

Why would someone engage in this type of crime against you? You would report it as soon as you could. It can get criminals many decades in prison, and most criminals know this. What would justify such a risk? Do you keep tens or hundreds of thousands of dollars of cash or cocaine in your house? Most of these robberies are against known targets and are not random at all. The average non-criminal person is unlikely to become a victim of one.

When professional groups do home invasion robberies, homeowners will rarely be able to use their guns to stop them. They happen too fast. Criminals doing home invasion robberies do not slowly creep into a home. The criminals know their target is home in a typical home invasion robbery. They intend to confront and compel the homeowner to tell them where their illegal money and drugs are hidden. You can expect a group doing home invasion robberies to have everyone at gunpoint within a second or two.

Unless you are wearing a gun and are immediately ready to draw and use it within a second or two, having a gun in the general area will not work in a robbery. Trying to stop an event like this by trying to find and arm yourself with a firearm will increase the risk of getting shot and killed.

In over 25 years of police work, I was called to only a few home invasion robberies at non-criminal households. In every case I investigated, the bad guys mistakenly hit the wrong house. They left the home quickly, realizing there were no drugs or cash to steal. If the owners had tried to arm themselves, the homeowner would likely have been shot and killed.

There may be reasons to consider getting a gun or arming yourself to protect your home or family but defending against the risk of a home invasion robbery is not a sound reason.

Military Assault-style firearms, one with a silencer.

CHAPTER FOURTEEN

BASIC TYPES OF MODERN FIREARMS FOR SALE TODAY

The descendants of ancient discoveries involving gunpower and firearms now come in three basic categories: Smooth-Bored Firearms, Rifled Firearms, and Shotguns.

Smooth-Bored Firearms

Other than shotguns, firearms without rifling in the barrel are called muskets or sometimes just smoothbores. Old-fashioned "black powder" firearms had smooth bores and were nowhere near as accurate as later rifles. Modern black powder firearms now have rifling in the barrel for accuracy, but like their historical antecedents, they can only fire one shot at a time. They do not use a shell to hold the gunpowder and the bullet. Instead, gunpowder is poured down the barrel, followed by wadding, then the bullet is tamped down with a ramrod. These weapons are slow to operate and are seldom used in criminal activity today. Think of someone in a raccoon skin hat with buckskin pants and a shirt with fringes, like in the old movies, and you get the idea.

Flintlocks were smooth-bored firearms that used a piece of hard stone, flint, on a lever that, once you pulled the trigger, struck a piece of steel to set off a spark that ignited and fired the weapon. Flintlocks are mostly museum pieces today.

Black powder guns are primarily used for target shooting or for hunting in special limited seasons.

Rifled Handguns and Rifles

Rifled handguns and long rifles fire a bullet that travels down a barrel with "rifling," or twisting grooves cut into the metal of the bore. The rifling makes the bullet spin and travels straight. Rifling works on the same principle as a gyroscope: Something spinning when traveling through the air does not change course without some other force acting on it.

Rifles vary from single-shot hunting rifles to those shooting 40 or more rounds in a clip in fully automatic military-style assault weapons. Similarly, handguns come in single-pull one-shot-at-a-time revolvers, to semi-automatic handguns that can also be made to fire fully automatically.

BASIC TYPES OF MODERN FIREARMS FOR SALE TODAY 103

Long Gun. This term refers to the length of a firearm's barrel but is also generally used to mean a rifle. There is little functional difference between a rifle and a rifled handgun outside the barrel's length and the stock. A long and rifled weapon is more accurate than a shorter one. A carbine is just a firearm shorter than a standard rifle and longer than a handgun, shoulder-fired like a hunting rifle.

Double Action Handguns. Handguns fire a single round each time you pull the trigger. With a double-action handgun, you pull the trigger until the hammer returns and then falls, driving the firing pin into the bullet. You do not have to cock this gun to fire it because that happens automatically when you pull the trigger. These are the most common handguns today. A new bullet is advanced into the firing position each time you fire. They are "semi-automatic."

Single Action Handguns. Some older or cheaper pistols are "single-action" handguns. When you pull the trigger, nothing happens. First, you must pull the hammer back and lock it into place, cocking the gun. Then you can pull the trigger and fire the weapon.

Many older or historic handguns are of a single-action variety. It is amusing that in many Western movies, handguns are single-action weapons (think of seeing the cowboy in a movie fanning the hammer with the trigger pulled). Still, they magically fire double-action and usually fire many more rounds than any revolver could hold. With each shot, this weapon also advances a new bullet into the firing position.

Revolvers. The action of a revolver includes a round cylinder containing five or six bullets. It turns after each shot, advancing the next bullet into the chamber in line with the firing mechanism and the barrel. You can fire all five or six bullets before having to re-load.

Derringers. Some handguns typically hold only one bullet or sometimes have two barrels that each fire one bullet, in either case, with a single trigger pull. They are called "derringers," a common misspelling of their patented action by the Deringer company. They are notable for being very small and concealable. They can fire many different types of rounds of ammunition, from very tiny to huge and powerful. In Western movies, these are the pistols that you will see professional card players wearing with retracting mechanisms up their sleeves. When somebody accuses the gambler of cheating, he trips the concealing mechanism, the pistol drops into his hand, and he aims it around the card table as he scoops up the money and runs. These weapons are notoriously inaccurate beyond a few feet but can still be deadly: A Deringer was the pistol that John Wilkes Booth used to assassinate Abraham Lincoln. Women like derringers because they are light and concealable, but they are a terrible choice for self-defense because they are so inaccurate beyond a foot or so and easy to wrestle from the owner.

Shotguns

Shotguns are smooth bored long firearms that usually fire pellets, not bullets. Shotguns can also fire a massive single projectile, called a slug, but more commonly, they fire multiple pellets available in varying sizes in a shell, or "load." The pellets inside the shell are contained in a plastic "wad" that keeps them together until they leave the shotgun's barrel. That inside plastic wad opens when it hits the air, and the individual projectiles spread out as they travel forward, spreading further apart as they fly. The plastic usually drops harmlessly not far from the muzzle of the shotgun.

A slug fired from a shotgun can also be rifled to travel in more of a straight line, but because they travel much more slowly than a rifle bullet, they are not good at shooting for long distances. In shorter distances, they are powerful and can shoot through a car or several walls or metal structures.

"Buckshot" is among the largest of the common multiple projectiles fired from a shotgun, and a standard 12-gauge shotgun's load of #00 Buck usually contains about nine large pellets. They can quickly kill people and large animals. By contrast, bird hunters use shotguns with much smaller size pellets but with many more pellets per casing.

The "gauge" of a shotgun refers to the diameter of the barrel and the type of shell it fires. The biggest is a 10 gauge, followed in descending order by the 12-, 20-, and 410-gauge shotguns. Gauge is determined by the number of lead balls of size equal to the approximate diameter of the bore that it takes to weigh one pound. For example, 12 lead balls with the same diameter as a 12-gauge shotgun bore would weigh one pound.

Shotguns are classified into single or double-shot, pump-action, and automatic varieties, describing how they are cocked and fired. The single or double-shot variety often breaks (bends open) in the middle when a button is pressed, ejecting the last used-up round or shell. You must then insert the new round into the chamber and close it before firing. Sometimes this cocks the trigger, and sometimes it must be cocked again before firing. Some have two triggers to fire either one or both barrels at once.

Other shotguns are loaded from the bottom or side. You can put several rounds or shells into the holding mechanism, where they will wait until the gun is "racked" or reload the next one into the chamber to fire it. In the case of an automatic shotgun, reloading happens automatically each time a round of ammunition is fired.

For police work, when I carried a shotgun, which I often did in hazardous situations, I always had some loads of #00 buckshot and a few slugs at the ready. For many tactical situations, this was often my ultimate weapon of choice. They can kill someone quickly.

People who are aficionados always love some certain gun. It's like their favorite sports team or car brand that can do no wrong. Although I could generally fire a perfect or near-perfect score at any standard police firing range, I have never been a gun nut. I have always seen firearms as tools for hunting or work. If I suggest a gun or type of gun, it is based on my personal experience. I can promise you that for everything I say in this book, someone out there loves guns and will disagree vociferously with my suggestions or comments. Don't let that bother you. Their experiences are not the same as mine. There is always an exception to every rule, and there are no perfect answers to choosing a firearm for any certain situation. Still, I know what I am talking about and have the practical experience to back it up.

CHAPTER FIFTEEN

CHOOSING YOUR FIREARM

There are thousands of firearms available in America today, so let's look at some you might want to think about to either purchase and use or to understand better.

To begin with, if you are buying a gun to store in case a dictatorship someday overthrows our country, then your selection might be different from a firearm purchased today for home defense. I address that in the chapter "What to Hide and Where to Hide It." In this chapter, I will discuss firearms selected for home defense.

Part 1 of 4 - All Quiet on the Western Front—The Rifle
On the night of June 24, 1982, I was sitting in a bedroom closet in a house in a rural area southeast of Seattle. I was with a police sergeant from another agency, and we were waiting for a man named Robert Hughes to return to his home in the dark. Earlier that day, Hughes had shot King County Sherriff's Deputy Samuel Hicks as he and another deputy drove up to the Hughes home to talk to him about a murder investigation. Detective Hicks was hit in

the abdomen with a .308 rifle from a distance away. The deputies turned their vehicle around and left the scene, but the wound was mortal, and Hicks died on the way to the hospital.

Local law enforcement officers went on a stake-out to catch Hughes. He had fled on foot. My partner and I were dropped off so there would be no vehicles near the house to give away our presence. That was a long night for me, hiding in a closet with my shotgun (you will notice, not a rifle.) Hughes did not return to the house that night. He had buried himself in nearby woods, where he had pulled leaves over himself to conceal his location. A police K-9 dog smelled him and alerted the handlers the next day. That's where he was arrested without firing shots or hurting anyone else.

The point here is to illuminate the danger and the utility of what police officers call a long gun or what most people think of as a hunting rifle. At any distance over 50 yards, nothing is a match to a rifle with a scope, a good rest to prop it on, and some cover or concealment. One person with a hunting rifle and a scope could hold off a small army. A single-shot bolt action rifle with a scope is the most devastatingly accurate firearm at more than 100 yards, especially if it is shooting high-velocity medium-caliber bullets. All the handguns, un-scoped AR-15s, and shotguns worldwide are no match at longer distances.

People considering buying a firearm for self-defense in their homes seldom think of a hunting rifle. This is partly because of the popular concept that military-style assault weapons are what everyone else has and that you need all those bullets for self-defense, but this is an error.

Rather than using an automatic weapon in a hostage or barricaded suspect situation, law enforcement generally will try to deploy a sniper with a long rifle and a scope. This is the only way to ensure accuracy, and the sniper seldom fires more than one single shot to end the encounter.

SPECIAL BULLETIN

DATE 06-25-82   CASE NO.

DEPARTMENT OF PUBLIC SAFETY
KING COUNTY POLICE
KING COUNTY COURTHOUSE
SEATTLE, WA 98104

HOMICIDE SUSPECT - ARMED & DANGEROUS

WARRANT #53669, SEATTLE DIST., MURDER 1° - BAIL $250,000.00
WILL EXTRADITE ANYWHERE IN UNITED STATES

HUGHES, ROBERT WAYNE
WM, 10-01-52, 6'2", 220#, blnd/blu
SCARS: Upper right arm tattoo removed; small scar under left eye; large scar right elbow.
TATTOO: Upper left arm of roses.
LKA: 22917 SE 380th; Kent, Washington
FBI: 283 820 J4
FINGERPRINT: 17 0 25 W   I00
             L 18 U 001 19
POB: Washington

HUGHES is wanted for the homicide of a King County Police Sergeant on 06-24-82 at about 1150 hours. At that time HUGHES was the prime suspect in the shooting death of a JOHN T. EARLY.

HUGHES was armed with an H & K .308 semi-automatic rifle which he discarded in a wooded area near the shooting scene of the police sergeant. It is unknown if HUGHES is still in possession of other weapons. He is known to be a woodsman and a survivor and most often carries a knife and/or handgun.

Wanted Poster for Robert Wayne Hughes June 25th 1982

The history of what you might think of as a "sniper" goes back at least 150 years in the U.S. During the Civil War, snipers got good at killing soldiers at long distances. One documented kill happened at over 4,000 feet, just under a mile, during the battle at Fort Sumpter in April 1861. Modern military snipers have documented kills at 10,000 feet or nearly two miles. Long single-shot firearms are dangerous and accurate weapons.

Military snipers have become adept at using rifles as powerful as .50 caliber weapons with high accuracy. Civilians can now buy these weapons if they want to. I see them occasionally in the woods, but they are costly to shoot, and untrained private citizens can injure themselves with severe head wounds due to their recoil. Two years ago, I saw an unprepared shooter fire a .50 caliber scoped rifle out in the woods. The recoil drove the scope into his head, splitting his scalp and underlying tissue and causing profuse bleeding. He was unconscious for several minutes, then affected by concussive brain trauma. You would never need a rifle this powerful for any reason.

Although I have pointed out that movies and the internet are the worst possible places to get accurate information about firearms, a scene in the famous 1930 WWI book and film, "All Quiet on the Western Front," is accurate. It is the final scene of probably one of the best anti-war movies ever made. At the movie's beginning, young German students are fooled into leaving school and signing up to fight in the German army. Initially, they are excited to go to war, but they eventually learn the realities of war, and by the end of the movie, they are all dead. A sniper kills the final soldier in this original group with a long rifle as he is reaching out just beyond the berm of his trench.

A close friend recently told me, "My dad's childhood buddy was killed by a sniper in Germany just after peace had been declared at the end of WWII." The sniper saw this exposed soldier and had not received the notice of hostilities ending. Exposure, when a sniper was in the area, could mean almost instant death in combat due to the accuracy of rifles.

An advantage to using a hunting rifle for home defense is that it is much less likely to be stolen from a home than a handgun or military-style assault weapon. Young people, gangs, and burglars seldom want them. They are too unwieldy to transport in secret and are not easy to sell for much. This alone makes them safer to have in a home. A bolt action hunting rifle is far more accurate at 100 to 300 yards than a handgun and even more accurate than an AR-15 automatic assault-style rifle without a scope. Hunting rifles also shoot bullets that expand when hitting a person and do extensive damage with a single shot.

What type of hunting rifle might be suitable for protection in your home? Anything that can accurately kill a deer, moose, or elk would work well in killing a person. Many older WWI and WWII surplus weapons are on the market, and people have hunted with them for decades. They tend to be larger caliber, like a .308 or 30-06. You can tell they are old because they have wooden rather than plastic stocks. I would avoid older, worn-out weapons from this era because many overused ones have worn-out rifling, so they are no longer accurate. A good gunsmith can tell you if they are still operable and safe.

Modern hunting rifles are often of smaller caliber but use a higher velocity bullet, or "round." Most are single-shot bolt-action rifles that are reliable and seldom misfire, but some come in semi-automatic versions. One such firearm is called a .270 Winchester round. Another is a .243. The .270 and .243 are not specific rifles; they are named for the bullets they fire. Different companies make rifle models that fire this .270 round, costing about $350 to over $1,000. Some are made with synthetic stocks, which are simple and virtually indestructible.

A hunting rifle is also practical because of how the bullet performs after it leaves the firearm's muzzle. Hunting rifle bullets come in different weights, but one of the most popular is the 130-grain round which travels at around 3,000 feet per second when measured at the muzzle. Their velocity makes them excellent for shooting long distances—they reach their targets before gravity has time to bring them down--but are also very powerful at close range. Standard hunting rounds of ammunition have soft points; a single one will cause significant damage if used in self-defense at close range.

Part 2 of 4 – A Shotgun Approach

The most terrifying sight that an intruder in your home will ever see is the muzzle of a shotgun aimed at the center of his chest. A single shot will be unsurvivable. If he has come to kill you, it is the last thing he will ever see. It makes no difference what he is armed with. There will be no shootout, just a killing.

The short range and width of the blast from a shotgun will obviate the inaccuracy of aiming a rifle or handgun when you are scared. Just point a shotgun in the right direction; if you can pull the trigger, you will kill everybody in its deadly path.

A considerable setback to using a shotgun is collateral damage from its blast. That is why police do not use shotguns in shopping malls, schools, or other crowded situations. This is less of an issue in your home or a confined situation. Probably not one at all.

I often carried a 12-gauge Mossberg stainless steel Marine Corps shotgun while carrying dangerous search warrants. Today, Mossberg sells a Tactical 590A1 model that the police and military often use. They are the ultimate tactical weapon, and even their presence convinces people that resistance or shooting back is pointless.

Another benefit of using a shotgun for home safety is that it is easier than other firearms to learn how to use. After some basic training, you point and shoot. There is no scope to keep sighted in or knock out of alignment. Well-made shotguns are resilient and resistant to climate and corrosion.

Firing 00 Buckshot, a 12-gauge shotgun, is a weapon that can stop anything or anyone in its path within 50 yards. In the 20' hallway of your home, nothing will survive it. This weapon has "knockdown" power. It can pick up the bad guy, throw him back a distance, and flatten him on his back. No one shot this way will be firing back at you.

Shotguns are not a weapon of choice for self-defense for most people, but they are the ultimate home defense weapon. They are not considered cool, and street gangsters don't want to be seen with them. They are seen as stodgy, akin to your grandfather's old duck-hunting gear.

The first person I saw killed with a 12-gauge shotgun was in 1983 when I was a police officer for the North Slope Borough Department of Public Safety in Alaska. I had only been there for a week and got a call about a shooting in an apartment. At that time, we had shootings and gun calls frequently. Barrow was likely the homicide capital of the known world at that time. We arrived at the scene and had to sneak down a long hallway. This was scary on a gun call, but each doorway was indented a little, so we did have some cover along the way. We were looking for a room halfway down the hall, so it was not a straightforward approach.

Coming to the door, I used a small round rear-view mirror like the one from a car to look inside. I didn't want to get shot through a doorway, sticking my head around a corner to look. My two partners and I probably took 10 minutes to approach the door and found it unlocked. I lay flat on the floor while my partners covered me. I reached the mirror around and inside the door. I could see a person lying on the floor and no one else inside. Then the other two officers entered the room while I watched from my low point and covered them with my handgun. Once we determined that the shooter was not inside, we found the guy on the floor, dead from a shotgun wound to the center of his chest.

Interestingly, the killer had tried to kill two of us about an hour earlier. Barrow had a severe alcohol problem back then, and drunks would try to ambush the police. It was almost like a local sport. All our Chevy Suburban patrol vehicles had bullet holes except one, too new to be shot up. People shot police vehicles so often that we just put square pieces of blue tape over the bullet hole instead of repairing them. When I was in orientation a week earlier and was told about all the square blue tape pieces on the vehicles, I thought my trainers were kidding me until I looked under the hood. Seeing the bullet holes from the inside, I found that it was true. I also found big cardboard boxes with black rubber things in them in the back of the patrol vehicles. When I asked what they were, I was told they were body bags. Again, I thought they were kidding. I'd never seen a body bag up to that point in my career.

Earlier, we had gotten a call that was like so many others. They went like this: The police dispatcher would answer a call, and the caller would say, "Send one quick!" The dispatcher would ask who was calling, and the caller would say, "You know who this is!" The dispatcher would say that she did not know (this was long before caller ID) and ask again for the caller's name. The caller would say their name and the dispatcher would ask the caller's location. The caller would answer, "You know where I live!" as if shocked that the dispatcher did not already know. The dispatcher would ask again, "Where are you calling from?" Because there were no street or house signs, the answer could be somewhat convoluted. Once the dispatcher established a location, she'd ask what the problem was, and the caller would hang up.

This was usually an ambush. Typically, an officer approaching the door would face several drunk people with hunting rifles who would then shoot. Even driving up to the house would get us shot, or at least we would need more pieces of blue tape for the bullet holes in the vehicle. We would sneak up on foot to the house and watch until someone walked away, and once he or she was safely away from the door or windows, we'd ask if everything inside was okay. If the answer were yes, we would cancel the call and go on to something else.

In this case, the bad guy got tired of waiting to shoot my partner and me and went to the house of the superior court judge to kill him instead, but the judge was on vacation in Hawaii. Now, even more frustrated, the shooter went to the apartment of his ex-brother-in-law, whom he disliked, and found the brother-in-law drunk on the floor, so he shot him in the chest with a 12-gauge shotgun. He shot at close range with birdshot, a popular goose and duck hunting round. The victim probably never even knew he was shot. The birdshot cartridge opened upon entering his chest, and the shot spread throughout his body cavity and went to his back. But since it was only birdshot, it did not pierce his skin and exit out his back. When we rolled him over, we saw a one-foot circle of small bumps of birdshot inside his skin. Everything else inside his chest was liquid mush that poured out the hole in the front of his chest when we rolled him over.

Once we completed our investigation, the Sergeant told me to get a body bag out of the back of the Suburban. They were not kidding about that. I soon found that we used them all the time. I inquired if a doctor or medical examiner should come and pronounce the person dead. The Sergeant said, "Are you stupid? You can't see that this guy is dead?" This seemed logical enough, albeit different from my earlier law enforcement experience in Washington State, where a medical examiner had to pronounce someone dead. I got a body bag from the vehicle, and we zipped the guy up inside. We dragged him down the stairs, stuffed him into the back seat of the patrol vehicle, and took him to the hospital in Barrow. We put him into their freezer so he could be sent to Fairbanks the following day for an autopsy.

In my year on the North Slope of Alaska during 1983 and 1984, I had more tactical shooting and dead body calls of one sort or another than most cops would ever get in an entire career in the lower 48. The excellent salary attracted many officers, but some lasted less than a day or two when they found out what our work was like. Some toughed it out and did their year, which is what the North Slope Borough Department of Public Safety asked of the officers they hired. A small number stayed and never left. It was a great place to observe the natural world but also a sadly brutal world of drugs and alcohol that devastated an ancient culture of people confronted with all aspects of middle-class American civilization at once. Over time, locals made possession and sales of alcohol a crime, and that helped.

Part 3 of 4 —What's an AR-15 and Why Not to Buy One for Home Defense

An AR-15 is a rifle initially designed and manufactured by the Armalite Rifle Company. Colt now owns the trademarked name, "AR-15." Its patents that form its design have expired, so other manufacturers may copy its design but can't use that exact name. In their advertising, they have to say "AR-15 style" firearm or words to that effect. The name is reserved for the trademark owner, like "Scotch Tape" for the 3-M company, but "mending tape" for other makers, or "Daisy BB Gun" for Daisy Outdoor Products, but "Daisy-like BB gun" for others.

The AR-15-style gun isn't just a single rifle. The name refers to a large group of weapons that most commonly fire the 5.56x45mm round or the .223 Remington cartridge. It can be chambered for many other rounds as well. There are also 25 different models of this weapon made by at least 15 companies. Many owners buy a long list of modifications from online retailers that allow them to turn these weapons into virtually thousands of different individual styles. Building a new one with parts from various sources from online sites is a common way of making a firearm without

Military assault-style firearms come in thousands of individual variations. They are not a single firearm. One here has a bipod attachment for stabilization and a laser sight, along with a scope on each.

background checks. Today there are hundreds of websites encouraging and explaining how to do this.

Between 1994 and 2004, sales and possession of military assault-style firearms were illegal. Then the law expired, and these weapons became available to anyone legally purchasing firearms. One of the most popular guns in America today is the formerly banned AR-15-style military assault-style weapon. The Russians and Chinese have their versions, like the AK-47 and the SKS.

Some years ago, the Israeli Uzi was all the rage, and everyone wanted one. The Uzi is a short, compact submachine gun. Many people thought it was the standard issue weapon for the Israeli army, but it was not. I have shot these at a firing range. I tried ones we took from bad guys, and I found them remarkably inaccurate at distances beyond a few feet. They became popular because you could spray 1,500 rounds a minute with them. And, of course, they looked cool. Please make no mistake; they can be dangerous, but you will generally hit more non-target things and people with one than you intended to hit.

The AK-47 became the standard of the automatic weapon industry around the world. In 1947, the inventor, Mikhail Kalashnikov, managed to create a weapon that could be dropped on the roadside, buried in the mud for several weeks, run over by a Jeep, and somehow still come out firing most of the time. It didn't matter what happened to them; they kept working. Around the same time, in the early 1950s, American military assault weapons were prone to breakdowns and performed poorly in bad weather or muddy conditions. They needed constant attention to keep them firing. Armies around the world preferred the AK-47 to American models. They still do today, and so do criminal street gangs in America. They loved the perceived simplicity and reliability over the American-made weapons, although current American models are more reliable than the older ones.

AK-47s are also much cheaper than American-made fully automatic weapons. The Russians made a gazillion of them in the early days, then chambered them to accept NATO ammunition, reportedly so they could fire any cache of ammunition captured from NATO members. This makes much sense in war. Ak-47s are easy to find and buy. There are estimated to be over 100 million of them today, and in 2012, Americans were buying far more than AR-15s. For a while, it was all the rage to own one.

The SKS was designed as a semi-automatic weapon only and made by the Russians. It is generally seen as an inferior weapon to the AK-47. The Chinese made and shipped over 15 million of them. They are inexpensive and easy to find.

"Military-style assault-type" weapons are deeply polarizing to Americans. Some people love them, and others see them as the poster child of what is wrong with American gun culture and crime. Emotion tends to replace facts in this debate.

"Military assault-style weapons" are primarily offensive weapons designed to kill or injure groups of people quickly, especially in some of the ways that Americans modify them after they leave the factory. Interestingly, it is not assault-style weapons but handguns used in many shootings in America today. However, that has been shifting in the last year towards more assault weapons because so many more are in the hands of Americans today. Although not as common, the most notable use of military assault-style weapons in a mass shooting was in Las Vegas in 2017. The accuracy of these weapons, especially when fired in full auto mode, is not high. Even seven or eight rounds being fired each second will be amazingly inaccurate, except when firing into a crowd of people. Hitting many people crammed into a dense crowd does not mean this is an accurate weapon. In crowded places, they are devastatingly deadly, even though they are usually inaccurate in the hands of most private American owners. Their danger comes from the amount of lead they can spray in a concise amount of time. They are dangerous weapons in the hands of untrained people.

People think that the more bullets a weapon has, the better it will be, but if you need more than the first two bullets, you are at a significant disadvantage and are now very likely to lose the encounter. That is how police are trained. At close range, they fire two shots at center mass (the middle of a person's upper torso) and assess whether the threat is neutralized.

Unlike in the movies, law enforcement officers do not empty a 30 or 40-round clip with a fully automatic firearm at longer ranges. Neither does the military. If they did, they would rarely hit anything, no matter how many rounds they fired.

Automatic weapons are devastatingly dangerous in the hands of police officers or military members who train with them often. You would not want to oppose a Navy Seal Team member or Army Ranger with one in a dark building. Your chances of surviving or winning that encounter would be slim to none. However, your peril is not due to the weapon but rather to the sophisticated training and discipline of the shooter.

An AR-15 is designed to be an offensive weapon, not a defensive one for home protection. Police wouldn't use them to defend their police stations from the inside like a home. They would use a shotgun for that.

AR-15-style weapons are expensive to shoot because they can fire so many rounds quickly, especially if they are fully automatic. Most of these weapons on full auto cost at least $3.50 per second (That's $210.00 per minute) to shoot cheap ammunition. Using much of this cheaper ammo will destroy the weapon in a short amount of time. Better ammo is twice that price.

Further, the skills necessary to be proficient with one of these will take more time and work than most Americans are willing to invest. I define "proficiency" as a level of knowledge and comfort that allows no mistakes in handling a tactical encounter against an armed person. More straightforward firearm options require less training, attention, and money for home defense.

Once a bullet leaves the muzzle of a firearm, it does not care what it has been fired from. It's just a bullet traveling through the air. Its accuracy and deadliness depend not on how many bullets are back in the gun behind it. Ultimately, all that matters is getting it into the air and determining where it will land. In the right hands, an AR-15-style assault weapon is a deadly offensive weapon, but good ones are expensive and more complicated to use and maintain.

Suppose your goal is to buy and possess an offensive weapon to give to a militia or a resistance operation against a dictatorship in the future. In that case, some of these might be very useful, and I will discuss how to acquire and store them in the chapter called "What to Hide and Where to Hide It."

Part 4 of 4 – Handguns

Handguns for home defense are popular because many are small and easy to conceal. Some criminal organizations like to use them as murder weapons because they can be quiet at very close range and are small and concealable. But a .22, .32, .25, or other smaller caliber handgun, in my opinion, is worthless in self-defense situations at a range outside a couple of feet. Mostly, a .22 handgun will wound but not kill unless discharged directly into a person's skull at point-blank range. I have seen a .22 bullet shot into a person's head that passed through one side of the skull, and instead of going out the other side, just ran around the inside like a racetrack, doing damage on the way. Some automatic handguns are tiny. These smaller ones also fire small rounds and, being almost hopelessly inaccurate beyond a few feet away, may not do much damage.

At a few feet away from an intruder, a 9mm, .38 Special, or .357 magnum will be fatal with a single shot or two to the center body mass if the bullet hits the heart or lung area. They will also be very noisy. The .38 Special rounds, and even some 9mm ammunition, are not as effective at further distances.

I do not include photos of any of this because I don't think forensic pictures are necessary for you to understand. However, if you are interested or like to watch Crime Scene CSI or programs like that on TV, it is easy to look at the entrance, exit, head, heart, and lung wounds on TV programs or with a simple online search.

As a police detective, I found crime scenes fascinating. Investigating them was always an interesting part of my job. I was not alone in this. Crime scene programs have become some of the most popular shows on TV. I don't watch many of them nowadays because I have seen most similar scenes in person over my years in police work. But from what I have seen, I can tell you that many programs are pretty accurate; they must have tracked actual cases or had police and forensic scientific advisors. You are lucky you can't smell crime scenes on TV or online.

As a practical matter, a revolver will virtually never misfire. Pulling the trigger of a double-action handgun will shoot a round of ammunition in the direction it is pointed at every time. An automatic will usually work, but not unless it is maintained to a high standard.

The Model 66 and Model 19 Smith & Wesson .38 Special or .357 handguns with 4-inch to 6-inch barrels are two of the best revolvers ever made. Police often use the shorter 2.5-inch barrel models in undercover roles because they are easily concealable but are still very powerful. These were carried by the FBI in years past. A .357 is chambered like a .38 Special so you can shoot either bullet from the same gun. One bullet is just shorter and less powerful than the other.

The Smith & Wesson Model 66 Combat Magnum with a 4.25-inch barrel, is the world's most accurate and reliable handgun. It is stainless steel and can come with a synthetic or tactical grip. This makes it easy to hold onto in all weather conditions. It is virtually indestructible and fires 100% of the time. I carried one during much of my police career. I could almost always shoot a perfect or very close to a perfect score on a police shooting range with one. Nothing else came as close. I also often carried the 2.5-inch Model

19 Smith & Wesson revolver when I wanted something more concealable or when I was working undercover. I could wear it in an ankle holster. It could also fire both the .38 Special and .357 magnum rounds. Although less accurate than the Model 66, in some cases, like in undercover work, it was much easier to have on my person or close by when I did not want it discovered or seen.

Advocates of automatic handguns will tell you that they are superior weapons. This is not always the case. Don't get me wrong, there are many fine semi-automatic handguns, and in full disclosure, I also carried one: A German-made Heckler & Koch .40 caliber S&W handgun. I carried it in my last few years as a detective commander. I had several police-issued 12-round clips that carried a particularly nasty hollow point round that was only available to law enforcement then. This was the most accurate and reliable semiautomatic handgun that I ever shot or carried, but in the end, I could outshoot it every time with my Model 66 Smith & Wesson revolver at a range. Both are excellent offensive and defensive weapons.

In years past, I had been issued 9mm semiautomatic police firearms, but personally deemed earlier versions inadequate for police work. Whenever I could get away with it, like many other knowledgeable police detectives, I put it away and carried better weapons. Detectives could usually get away with this, but often patrol officers could not; most detectives had different rules and flexibility on what weapons they carried if they had qualified adequately with them at the range and would maintain them.

I can't tell you how often I saw or had 9mm police handguns jam or misfire. Newer ones are better than those early ones. The early 9mm Glock was the worst, which I considered almost entirely worthless. Many guys loved them. I think primarily because they were deemed to be cool. Of all the hair-brained ideas, Glock put the safety in the trigger to make it easier to fire. Once the trigger was partly pulled, the safety, a small lever in the trigger, released as the trigger returned, allowing the gun to be fired. That was unlike conventional safeties that lock the internal parts of the firearm from a lever away from the trigger, on the outside of the action. Having the safety of a handgun in the trigger is a bad idea.

The older 9mm Glocks caused too many workplace injuries and death claims, and after several police officers were killed with their service weapons in quick succession, many were removed from police work.

A proper handgun should have a safety that is difficult for a bad guy to figure out quickly (if it has one, many do not). If they got my H&K away from me, if the safety were on, it is doubtful that they could have gotten it to fire in less than a minute or two. On that gun, the user must look at, read, and understand the message on the side to get it to work.

I once visited a good friend in police work at his office and noticed that he had a hand grenade on his desk. Looking closer, I could see a big dent in the front that looked like the shape of a bullet. My friend was a commander but also a SWAT team member. I asked him about the item. He told me that "Chuck," another member of his SWAT team, a good friend of each of us, had accidentally shot him with a live round during training at Fort Lewis, a local Army facility.

The bullet hit the hand grenade that was hanging on his ballistic vest. Even though all guns had to be carefully "cleared" before the exercise, meaning they had to have no live rounds, Chuck left a bullet round in his semi-automatic handgun and accidentally fired it. Chuck, who had been a military sniper, was famous for taking "headshots" at close range, which was discouraged in police work and not often done because a person's head is a much smaller target than the center body mass in the chest area. Fortunately, this was not a headshot. Instead, the bullet hit the hand grenade, smashing it without setting it off and crushing it into the ballistic vest the Commander was wearing. No one was severely hurt, and there were repercussions for the accident, as there must always be in police work, but no one got fired. Even highly trained officers on a SWAT team can make mistakes with semi-automatic weapons. This could not have happened with a revolver. It did, however, make a great desk ornament!

Simplicity, reliability, proper caliber, and power far outweigh the need for more complex, higher-capacity firearms. Further, adequately trained persons with a revolver can re-load it almost as quickly as an automatic handgun with a device called a "speed loader." With speed loaders, I can re-load six bullets into a revolver in three seconds without looking and in about two seconds with visual contact.

Model 66 S&W .357 Combat Magnum w/4.25" barrel

CHAPTER SIXTEEN

WHAT TO HIDE AND WHERE TO HIDE IT

So, let us say you are concerned about a civil war by some Republicans or radical extremist groups or a takeover by a fascist regime or dictatorship, not unlike what Trump and his supporters attempted on January 6, 2021. You are not interested in a firearm for personal safety today but might want one to protect yourself or get your country back from a dictatorship and want one securely hidden for such a time. This was the original intent of the 2nd Amendment, America's defense against tyranny. There are many things to consider, and we will cover them in the following few chapters. It will not be possible later once such an event happens, as all citizens' access to firearms will be locked down and ended by the regime once they take power and are firmly in place.

Part 1 of 2 – Locations to Hide Weapons and Ammunition
If you are storing a firearm for some future militia or resistance purpose and are not going to open the box and fire it yourself, keep the original manual and any spare parts or cleaning kits with it, then make sure the storage container for your weapon is entirely watertight and closed to all outside elements for long-term storage. That can end your firearms training and preparation to be in the "resistance."

When I say "secure," I mean very secure. Large free-standing gun safes are not for this purpose. Everyone knows that gun safes hold guns. In the case of a dictatorship taking control of our country and its supporters coming to your house, a gun safe would be a sure sign that you had a gun and where you'd stored it.

The best place for a weapon for future use is locked up and hidden somewhere that no one can get into or even find in the first place. You would never want this type of weapon to get into the hands of anyone outside of its intended purpose. It would be best if no one even knew you had it. If a dictatorial regime searched it, you would also not want it to be found in your house.

Many weapons for the resistance hidden in WWII were buried in the ground. Some were built into walls in houses and were almost impossible to find. Those hidden improperly were discovered in searches, and their owners were often imprisoned or killed by the regime. Hiding something in your house so it cannot be found takes some work and thought.

One relatively simple way to hide a firearm is to open an existing wall, put the weapon and ammunition in, and then seal the wall with drywall to look like it did before the work began. The weapon would never be available for use without some difficulty and work. A magnet or metal detector would also not detect the weapon if this were done in areas with metal pipes or other structural metals in the building. Other surrounding metal can disguise the shape of a gun, even from X-rays. Inside or under cabinets can also be good hiding places once closed back up. This does not mean just putting them on the shelves but building them into areas not open for usual access and storage.

One of the best hiding places I ever saw was uncovered during a search warrant and concealed 15 ounces of contraband cocaine built into a pinball machine. We knew the drugs were in the house but could not find them. After hours of searching, we brought in a drug-sniffing dog named "Pounder," operated by a Seattle police officer. Within 10 minutes, Pounder sat at the front of the pinball machine, and sure enough, we found the cocaine. We would have never found it without the help of the drug dog.

Even when drugs are packaged carefully, they still give off an odor that dogs can detect. Guns are much harder to find because most dogs can't detect them. Properly cleaned guns with no burnt powder or residue odor are challenging to detect.

Part 2 of 2 – What to Hide - Packaging & Materials
Remember that it is useless without ammunition if you are hiding a weapon. 200 to 500 rounds are the minimum of what you might think of hiding along with the weapon, possibly divided into a couple of different locations, just in case one parcel is found. These items must be put into plastic bags and sealed from the elements, like heat, cold, moisture, and vermin.

Removing all the ambient air from the gun and ammo packages is essential. You can push or suck the air out once the plastic is sealed or use a leaf blower by plugging it into the sucking function. Food bag sealers that remove all the air are also great when packaging ammunition.

Other items, like a small brush on a long aluminum shaft to clean the inside of the barrel, are also necessary. A cleaning kit will be available for virtually any firearm when you purchase it. A broken or improperly maintained firearm will be unreliable and could become inaccurate, so I would place the owner's manual in plastic packaging and hide it. I would not keep the manual where it could be found because it strongly indicates that firearms are hidden in the house.

Burying and hiding weapons in the ground is an option, but you must ensure the packaging is entirely sealed against the elements. I'd start with a hard-locking plastic gun or metal case with an eggshell foam barrier inside, completely seal all edges of the outer gun case with epoxy and then a layer of silicone sealant, then package it in several successive layers of heavy plastic, also vacuum sealed.

Three different types of weapons might be helpful for future resistance situations. One is a long rifle that can shoot people from significant distances away. You might think of this as a sniper type of situation. Resistance organizations used these frequently against Nazis in WWII. Unfortunately, they often had to adapt and shoot old WWI military weapons that were not ideal. The bullets were large and powerful but traveled slowly and were brought down by gravity too quickly. Sometimes the barrels were "shot out," meaning that the rifling was so worn that the weapons were inaccurate.

Another concept affecting your choice is that a rifle needs to be extremely simple. There is nothing more straightforward and reliable than a bolt-action rifle. They can hold several rounds and fire one each time you use the "bolt" to eject a round and push another into the firing chamber. They will work in any condition or weather. They never jam or fail to fire, unlike semi or fully-automatic weapons that can notoriously be unreliable over time. The only limitation is that the weapon's scope must work properly and be on target.

This weapon will generally use a single shot to neutralize the target. After that, the person using it will leave the area as quickly as possible. That is how they were used in real-life situations in WWII in countries that the Nazis occupied.

To be accurate, a rifle needs a scope. There are two styles to consider. One is a variable distance scope with an eyepiece that you can twist to see different distances. This is often the best, as you may not know the distance you will be shooting for which you need an accurate image. However, extra moving parts can malfunction. The more complex the mechanism is, the more chances it has for something to go wrong or break. The alternative is a fixed distance scope that only magnifies at a single distance. Everything at any distance is clear, but you cannot "zoom" in.

The most reliable hunting scopes in the world are generally 4x scopes (4x means zoomed in 4 times closer), but they are not quite as good at longer distances. There are other fixed magnification scopes, but most today are variable. Their quality and reliability are often directly proportional to their price.

Regarding the numbers on scopes, in a 3-9x40 scope, the 3 means three power, or 3x. This means that the image you see through the scope appears three times (3x) closer than it does with your naked eye. With a fixed 4x, or 4 power scope, the image is four times closer, and you cannot change it or zoom in.

The 9x variable means nine power, or nine times (9x) closer than it appears with your naked eye. The forty (40) is the size of the diameter of the objective lens (at the front, far end of the scope from your eye) measured in millimeters. With a variable scope like this, you can dial in the distance you want to magnify.

I like Redfield Scopes, the ones that are made in the US. The 4x power wide-field fixed is one of my favorites. I can hit something reliably at 200 yards all day with this scope. It never drifts off target. It is a straightforward design and is ruggedly built.

Leupold scopes made in the U.S. are also high quality and reasonably priced. A 3-9x40 would be an excellent sniper scope, but they have more moving parts and will take more maintenance. The best option is to have two scopes, a fixed 4x scope and a 9x variable one. With two, you have a backup if one has a malfunction, and they can work in different situations.

A rifle with a scope cannot hit anything until the whole thing is "sighted in," which means that the scope is adjusted with some screws, so the image in the middle of the crosshairs in the scope is where the bullet hits. A person who is using the rifle is going to want to test the rifle and sight it in before using it. It might be best to buy a good scope, store it in its original box, and hide it away.

No scope will work without the proper scope mounts that hold the scope onto the weapon. Ensure you have at least one or two of these to fit the weapon and scope(s) you bought. Also, ensure you have the required tools or materials to attach the scope to the rifle. They will be explained in the instructions. Once correctly fitted, some can be left on, others can come off and back on quickly, and no tools are necessary.

Earlier, we talked about small and concealable handguns, and ones for tactical operations and shooting at close range at average handgun distances of several feet to up to 50 feet. Good handguns are reliable and do not need work, and only need cleaning to keep them firing. Package them in the original containers and seal them. If you are going to this much trouble, do not bother with older, used, worn, or handguns unless you know they are in excellent working condition.

You might ask about getting and storing an AR-15 or similar weapon. As you know, these are primarily offensive weapons instead of good defensive ones. As such, they can be helpful in warfare situations. Even a small number of them in the hands of skillful operators can be used to attack a group of people and be very successful. The Dutch underground would have loved a few of these for killing gatherings of Nazis during WWII. If you are storing one, there is a good chance someone with training and experience can use it. If you do not have the proper training and experience, don't plan on getting much of that experience and training after everything has gone wrong. If you are wealthy, you could buy several of these and store them, but I would not put them all in the exact location. Weapons and ammunition stored all in one place was a mistake made in WWII-occupied areas.

A shogun, such as a Mossberg 12-gauge Marine Corps stainless steel or the more modern Mossberg 590A1 Tactical, would be a devastatingly powerful defensive and offensive tactical weapon to store. There is nothing to match it at 50 yards or less in the right hands. In war, collateral damage is far less of an issue than using it against a shooter in a school or shopping mall today. At close combat distances, I would take one of these over a dozen AR-15s any day of the week. Get one and secure it.

You will probably want to know where to buy these firearms. Many larger chain outdoor stores no longer sell any military-style assault weapons. I also believe that there is a moral component to this type of purchase. Most competent and professional gun dealers do not wish to become political or illegally arm the wrong types of people. But not all of them. Check out the reputation of your local gun stores.

Many "Gun Shows" have been notoriously lax about putting weapons into the hands of anyone who wanted them, including criminals and mentally ill people, without doing background checks. I would not spend my money there.

You can ship rifles, but not handguns, by USPS. FedEx and UPS can ship them to people with federal firearms licenses. Most gun stores have this designation.

Again, the hope is that these hidden weapons and ammunition would never be necessary for America. If you had suggested this as a good idea to me in 2014, I would have thought you were nuts. But not anymore. Most people I know today understand that the risk of a dictatorship taking over America is no longer an entirely fantastical delusion and that Trump is not the only person who might lead people to such an end.

Finally, always check and comply with your local and state laws when acquiring any firearm.

CHAPTER SEVENTEEN

FIGHT CLUB FOR DEMOCRATS

What is the first rule of "Fight Club"? If you've seen the movie, of course, you know that the first rule of Fight Club is that you never talk about Fight Club. The second rule about Fight Club? You never talk about Fight Club. This 1999 movie with Bran Pitt and Edward Norton is a great classic, but I remind you of it here because of the concept: When you purchase a firearm, whether, for yourself or others, <u>you don't talk about it.</u>

I am a big fan of Brad Pitt and some of the movies he has made about fighting and killing Nazis, like "Inglorious Bastards" or "Fury," and I enjoy his ideas of bringing Nazis to justice in various and creative ways. I like the scene where WWII ended early with one of the Nazis making a deal to help kill Hitler and his entire staff at a movie theater in occupied France. In truth, many German Army leaders attempted to assassinate Hitler but failed in all these plots. One of the most famous involved Lieutenant Colonel Claus von Stauffenberg on July 20, 1944, near Rustenburg in East Prussia. This group of conspirators is an excellent example of how people must operate in such cases. Their plan worked in blowing up the building that Hitler was in, but Hitler survived due to being behind a very thick wooden desk. However, the conspirators did carry it out without being detected. Secrecy was their ally.

The first thing any dictator will do after taking over America is to take away everyone's guns. Dictators always need to control all the guns themselves. If this happens, and anyone knows you have a gun, everyone else will know very quickly. You will lose it. Your plan will be worthless.

If you want a gun to protect or restore our American democratic republic, you should not tell anyone about it. Procure and store it so people do not know anything about it. It should be something you eventually forget about yourself over time until such an event occurs. It will be invaluable for such a purpose if adequately hidden.

An excellent book was published in 2021 called Three Ordinary Girls: The Remarkable Story of Three Dutch Teenagers Who Became Spies, Saboteurs, Nazi Assassins and *WWII Heroes* by Tim Brady. If you think you might face a situation such as a threat to American democracy, you might wish to read this book. It points out the dangers of people knowing the identities and resources of the resistance under a tyrannical dictatorship like Hitler's regime. The same thing happened in most other occupied countries in WWII. Although the Allies did their best to free the world of nationalism and radical racism during WWII, the people had to do more than wait for years to be rescued. Like these teenage girls and many others, brave people heeded the call to action. How the girls hardened and adapted to their situations is well explained. If even 1,000 Dutch people had made these types of secret preparations in advance and stored modern and operable weapons, they might have collapsed the Nazi regime in months, not years.

This is not to say that if such an event happens, you will be the person, like these girls, who will fight directly to restore democracy and civilized order. Only a few people did. These types of operations are not for everyone. But those who did were helped by scores of others in supporting roles who supplied arms, housing, intelligence, and other means of support to those fighters who took more significant risks than themselves. In this book mentioned above about the Dutch resistance, you can see that it took some work for the underground to get itself appropriately armed to support the Allies coming to liberate them. The in-country citizens loyal to the rule of law and running the resistance were critical to the Allied operations.

Throughout Europe and the rest of Nazi or Imperial Japanese-occupied areas, people quickly learned that they had to keep the secret of their hidden weapons to themselves. The more people talked, the more they were discovered, locked up, or killed.

If such a thing happens in America, what would be your role? If Democrats, Independents, Jews, and racial groups opposing a dictator were being systematically exterminated, what would you be doing? Was there a way to be neutral when fellow citizens were rounded up, placed into concentration camps, and exterminated by the millions during WWII? As much as we would like to think that nothing like this could ever happen in America, especially after WWII when we all fought to rid the earth of nationalism, and the Nazi party and nationalists in Japan, January 6th suggests that this could repeat itself once again here in America. Antisemitism is rising dramatically in America today, primarily driven by Trumpists and other white supremacist groups, and make no mistake about it – they are heavily armed.

You may have seen what seems to be a conflicting concept in this book. On the one hand, I have told you to keep your gun purchases secret. On the other hand, I have also said that if you acquire guns, then Trumpists will be less likely to attempt a coup again and install a dictatorship. One is individual, and the other is collective. Just because your gun purchase is private and not subject to public knowledge, if Democrats, Independents, and communities of color were getting guns and storing them in a big way, everyone would know it. Just like how we know who has been buying guns and arming themselves in the last decade and why they have done so. In Jimmy Buffett's speech, this is called the "coconut telegraph." People always know, and journalists always find the story, but it will be collective, not individual. Everyone will know if there are millions of guns in the hands of a new group but won't know whether you individually have one. Keep your gun purchases private for now.

My partner and I, & Ted Dahm in a booking photo & Cessna 182 N7380S, which was later lost in a crash.

CHAPTER EIGHTEEN

SNITCHES GET STITCHES

One of comedian Trevor Noah's favorite sayings is: "Snitches get stitches, baby; that's what I'm talking about." I laugh every time he says it. You may think this is a joke, but it is accurate on the street. It means that informants get what they have coming – stitches. Informants are a despicable lot, usually criminals themselves, that is true, but I used them in police work all the time.

With that in mind, who can you trust with information about your home defense weapon or involvement in the resistance to restore democracy if this came to pass? Your best friends? Your family? Your local political organizations or associates? None of the above. The real world is very different. Most insurgencies against a dictatorship learn very quickly that loose lips sink ships. Even a little pressure will get many people to tell everything they know. Some will provide information to show that they were trusted with it in the first place. People love to blab "secret" information. It's just what humans do.

I taught Advanced Narcotics Investigations and Informant Development classes for the Washington State Criminal Justice Training Commission and the United States Department of Justice. I specialized in American, Mexican, and Columbian organized crime drug investigations. American drug crime families are simple, and it is not difficult to turn informants from within these groups. We did it all the time. Mexican crime families used to be tough to break into but are not so today. Columbians were the most difficult for everyone in law enforcement for a very long time. They were smart. Before hiring you, they made you fill out a job application listing every extended relative you had. If you turned informer, they assured you they would hunt down and kill all of them to send a message to others who might think of doing the same.

One of the largest original cocaine smuggling organizations in the Seattle area was run by Ted Dahm. That was a very long time ago when cocaine was still new. He had a thriving business empire and was making lots of money, but his plan had a catch. He had to drive to Los Angeles and back each week with loads of cocaine. It was a bummer to drive and travel when he could have been using cocaine and cash with his friends, enjoying a high-priced lifestyle. We knew about him and his organization, and one day another detective and I hatched what we thought was a terrific plan. One of the lowest guys on his payroll had a suspended driver's license and an extensive history of criminal traffic violations. His record was enough to put him in jail for 90 days if caught driving. Generally, we couldn't flip an informant on such a chippy charge, but we also knew this guy had a phobia about jail and was a drug addict (which his boss did not know).

We arrested him while he was driving and told him about the 90-day jail term he was facing. He agreed to cooperate, just like that. We asked him if he knew any criminals, and he identified his boss, Ted Dahm, as a target. We acted surprised. We told him to tell his boss that he knew some pilots who were also crooks. My partner and I were both pilots. A couple of days later, we got a call from Ted, and he asked us how much it would be to fly to LA and back. We gave him a price, and he agreed. This would cut his travel time to LA and back by several days a week! Ted could not wait to have more fun in his spare time. It never dawned on him that a pilot might be a police detective. We ran this by our bosses, and they didn't see a problem with it. It is doubtful that such a plan would be implemented so quickly today without much more deliberation, but back then, things were simpler.

It was a blast. Just in case we were hijacked and were so close to Mexico and did not want to get tortured, we carried no ID. We duct-taped two handguns under the dash of the plane up in the front. If we were hijacked, our contingency plan was to fly around for a while and say we were lost, and then hand Ted Dahm a map and shoot him in the head with the gun concealed behind the map, shooting through the map. We figured that a bullet from either of our guns would go at such an angle that it would not hit any aircraft control devices in the tail and go out the side of the plane after it went through his head. This was probably not the best idea in the world, but it seemed a good idea at the time. We just knew there was no way we would allow ourselves to get tortured

GUN GUIDE FOR DEMOCRATS

Ted Dahm's $234,000.00 in cash, ten kilograms of cocaine, firearms, and silencers.

in Mexico. We also had a secret code to send using a radio transponder in the plane. If Air Traffic Control received it, the controllers would alert the military that something was wrong. They also had the numbers and codes to understand the message and call our units back in Washington State and California with further pre-arranged aircraft radio messages.

Ultimately, we flew Ted Dahm to California with $234,000.00 in cash. He bought 10 kilograms of pure cocaine worth nearly a million dollars in street value. He also picked up a load of illegal gun silencers from a machine shop in the LA area. We arrested him in Los Angeles on our second trip with him, and he was charged in Federal Court. This was a significant seizure of cocaine at the time. He was so shocked that his pilot "friends" were cops that he became catatonic for two days after finding out and could not speak.

The point of this story is how easy it is to flip people and get them to inform on their friends, associates, and even their family members. Think about the risk this guy took. The driver informed against a criminal organization that would have been more than happy to kill him for doing so, to avoid a driving violation and a little bit of local jail time. I could tell you hundreds of stories just like that one.

People swear they would never flip and inform against their friends, family, or associates, but they do it all the time. It is not that difficult to get someone to inform against others. There are countless motivations and psychological reasons why it is so easy. If you are in such a situation someday, the fewer people who know about your plans or involvement, the better.

I once arrested another guy, Randy Johnson, for running a drug enterprise who swore to his cohorts that they would never tell on anyone in their group, even if they were having their fingernails pulled out one at a time. Sounds painful. We knew about the promise due to a phone intercept when a digital phone recorder, or Pen Register, was installed on their phone. We thought it was funny. It was a large group, and when I arrested Johnson and took him to the prosecutor's office in Seattle for an interview, it only took 20 minutes before he gave up everyone, including his mother. She was part of his smuggling operation and made the trips from LA to Seattle in a Ford LTD because it had one of the enormous trunks of any car at the time.

Most people think they are too tough to snitch until they face legal pressure or personal gain. I can tell you that most people will do it. The only people who cannot inform against you are those who don't know about you in the first place.

A skillful investigator can get almost anyone to talk within about four hours of interrogation. I mean just polite discussion, not torture or good-cop bad-cop stuff like you see on TV. Torture does not get reliable information, nor does too much pressure. A person under pressure or pain will tell you anything you want to hear to feel better. Good interrogators don't need it.

I also learned that a detective could get a person, in some cases, to admit to a crime he did not even commit. For that reason, professional police investigators and prosecutors will always require corroborating evidence before charging someone based on a confession alone.

My point here is that if you are going to join the resistance against a dictatorial regime, you should not tell people about it who do not need to know, maybe not even many of your family members. Indeed, not any friends or associates who are not among a tiny number of highly trusted resistance members. These groups will be broken down into microscopic cells that do not know the identity of other ones. That will keep you, your weapon, and your involvement as secret and safe as possible.

By the time the "Troubles" ended in Northern Ireland (1968-1998), it was widely reported that nearly half of the members of the IRA were providing information to their opponents. Even higher numbers in the leadership were cooperating with the British or Northern Ireland Governments. Some good books on this subject are *Say Nothing* by Patrick Radden Keefe (2019) and *Rebel Hearts* by Kevin Tollis (2015). Barrack Obama recommended *Say Nothing*, and it is an excellent read. The title comes from the concept that if you ever talk to any investigators, they will get everything from you over time. Hence the idea, "If you say anything, say nothing." If you think a dedicated person in a political cause would never inform, read *Killing Rage* by Eammon Collins (1998), who details how it happened to him.

Another example is former Senator John McCain, a prisoner of war in Vietnam. Senator McCain was a great American hero, but under the pressure of torture, he talked to those imprisoning him. Most people would. No one is immune. Keep a plan like this to yourself, and do not tell others. No one can tell things about you that they do not know.

You might now ask when you should reveal what you have, whom to tell about it, and how to use it if necessary. Good question. There isn't a simple answer other than to say you will know it when the time comes. That is how these things work out. All voting and elections will have ended. Those not swearing loyalty to the regime will be arrested or "detained" and hauled off. Our judicial and legislative branches of government will be ended or compromised and not function independently. You and your friends will know what to do when the time comes. However, you should proceed with the utmost caution and deliberation until then.

November 10, 2017, Russian President Vladimir Putin, who very seldom smiles, with U.S. President Donald Trump. Alamy Stock Photo.

CHAPTER NINETEEN

~

O CANADA! & WAR IN EUROPE

Our neighbor to the north published a report on November 27, 2019, on its official Statistics Canada website, indicating the nation had 249 firearm-related homicides in 2018. Yet there are 34.7 firearms for each 100 Canadians in the nation. Canadians are familiar with firearms and have plenty of them, but they approach responsible firearm ownership differently than we do. America's firearm homicide rate per capita is almost triple that of Canada.

Canada has its problems, of course, as all countries do. But what is happening in America is now spilling over into Canada, as evidenced by truckers in February of 2022 who blocked routes from Canada to the US, causing hundreds of millions of dollars of damage to both economies. These illegal rioters flew Trump and confederate flags and were even openly supported by far-right American politicians like U.S. Senator Ted Cruz and others.

Dwayne Lich went to court in Canada and told the Canadian Judge at his wife's bail hearing that he and his arrested wife were exercising their "First Amendment rights," to which the judge responded, "Your what?" The first amendment to the Canadian constitution says: *"An Act to amend and continue the Act 32-33 Victoria chapter 3; and to establish and provide for the Government of the Province of Manitoba, 1870, 33 Vict., c. 3 (Can.)"*. In other words, this Canadian had never read the Canadian Constitution and didn't realize that the American Constitution does not apply to Canada. Espousing "First Amendment Rights" as a justification for committing crimes will not protect anyone arrested in Canada, let alone in the United States. Few Trump supporters in America have ever actually read or understood the Constitution.

Two recent stories out of Canada show how destabilizing the ascendency of Trump and his nationalists are and how the events of January 6th impact everyone. One is a book by Canadian author Stephen Marche called *The Next Civil War: Dispatches from the American Future*. He is asking Canadians to begin thinking of what it will be like when democracy ends in America and how this will impact Canada. The other is an op-ed by Thomas Homer-Dixon called *The American Polity is cracked and might collapse. Canada must prepare*. He is the Director of the Cascade Institute, a think tank. It was published in the Canadian newspaper, the *Globe and Mail*. It begins by suggesting that American democracy could collapse, causing extreme domestic political instability and widespread civil violence.

Both writers predicted that on our current course, democracy is likely coming to an end in America in the not-too-distant future. They also predict that a second American Civil War is now likely. The question for them is what to do if a Trumpian dictatorship begins demanding that Americans who oppose Trump be returned from Canada to America for punishment or even death. What will Canada do in such a case? How can they defend their democracy when ours unravels? What will they do to help Americans reclaim our democratic republic in such a case?

While I was drafting this book, Russia's Putin was massing troops and weapons on the border of Ukraine. The world held its breath, hoping that an invasion would not occur. Sadly, the invasion is underway, and for the first time in 77 years, Europe is now on the precipice of a world war. Not since the rise of Nazism and Adolph Hitler has anything on the potential of this scale occurred. There have been wars in Europe, and people in the Balkans (the general area of Albania, Bosnia and Herzegovina, Bulgaria, Croatia, Kosovo, Montenegro, North Macedonia, Romania, Serbia, and Slovenia) can attest to wars and genocide, but not since Hitler marched into Poland on September 1, 1939, has anything like this happened. Putin has threatened nuclear war if opposition to his efforts to overtake Eastern Europe goes too far.

Most of the world responded in shock, dismay, and condemnation against Russia and Putin for this war of conquest. But right after the invasion began, Donald Trump called Putin a "genius" for invading Ukraine and said that Putin could take the country "for only $2.00 in sanctions." He urged Putin that this was a bargain. He also called the United States stupid and dumb. Trump later tried to correct some of his pro-Putin statements, but in the first few days, he expressed his true feeling for Putin and the invasion of Ukraine. In the past, Trump offered his support for Putin's invasion of Crimea by saying that the people living there were better off being ruled by Russia, even though this was sovereign Ukrainian territory.

During his term, Trump tried to extort Ukraine by withholding military aid that the U.S. had promised Ukraine unless the country produced evidence of wrongdoing by Hunter Biden. Biden is the son of President Joe Biden, who was just a candidate opposing Trump at the time. Delaying weapons to Ukraine improved the position of Putin for this current invasion.

Trump would have never been elected without Putin's massive interference in our 2016 election. After studying the reports of investigations, I believe that the Trump campaign operatives were meeting and coordinating with the Russian disinformation campaign. As a result of the special counsel investigation, 34 people were indicted, although Trump himself has not been charged with a crime. During that period, Trump mused that Putin might be his best friend, and as recently as March of 2022, in a tape-recorded conversation with John Daly said, "You know, he was a friend of mine. I got along great with him."

Trump spent his four years in office doing everything he could to demonize, underfund, and undermine NATO, the North Atlantic Treaty Organization created after WWII to restrain the menace of the Union of Soviet Socialist Republics, dominated by Russia. Trump has made it clear how much he admires Putin personally, and Trump wishes to be a ruler in Putin's style.

So, here's why this all matters to Americans who are considering acquiring weapons to help preserve the American democratic republic. What is happening in Ukraine now is what dictators will do every time if they do not face the restraints of the democratic rule of law. If you want to know what a Trumpian dictatorship will look like in America when our democracy is gone, look at Russia and the war and suffering in Ukraine today. WWII in Europe directly resulted from the rise of fascism and the Nazis taking power. It is now a war crime in Russia for journalists or citizens to report on the fact that there is a war or criticize Putin publicly. People opposing Putin will receive 15-year prison sentences and go to work camps, or worse.

When Trump was president, how often did you hear him say that free and fair reporting by the media was fake news? How often did you listen to him talk about wishing he could get rid of the free press as Putin has in Russia? In a March 8, 2022, interview with Trump's former press sectary, Stephanie Grisham, on *The View*, she said, "Trump admired Putin for just being able to kill journalists."

If America falls to fascism, I fear for Canada and other democracies as well. They have good reason to be deeply concerned about a dictatorial regime in America. Putin is an example of a dictator who continuously attempts to expand their borders. If Trumpists ever took total power in America, they would try to expand America's boundaries. Mainstream news organizations in other countries are deeply concerned about our potential decline.

Trumpism is a belief system. It is not about just the man. Trump gave voice to white supremacists, anti-Semitics, and other radical nationalists who seek to end democracy and replace it with a dictatorship without constitutional restraints. Many others would be willing and able to lead this movement if Trump were gone or discarded, notably Ron DeSantis of Florida, but he is not the only one. In 2021, DeSantis proposed creating a massive new private army that would be answerable only to him in Florida, not unlike Germany's Brown Shirts of the 1930s, who answered only to Hitler. In 2023, DeSantis also demonstrated that he is willing to deploy loyalists against any person or company who opposed him when he attacked the Disney Company for speaking out against his "Don't Say Gay" law in Florida schools. He said he would put Disney out of business or build a prison next door to them to bend Disney to their knees in obedience to his will. The world heard this type of talk decades ago from Hitler in Germany before WWII. We must heed the lessons of the past or be condemned to repeat a horrible chapter in human history.

Our democracy is in peril. If given another chance at what they tried to do on January 6, 2021, Trumpists will not repeat the same mistakes. They might be successful next time if we do not stop them before they get the chance.

CHAPTER TWENTY

A THOUSAND EASY PIECES

You may feel that, as a country, we need to do more to protect our citizens from improper gun use and violence. I agree. Curiously, so do most gun owners in America. Although support for more stringent gun laws will tend to ebb and flow, depending on the media coverage of mass shootings, most gun owners believe that safety should be a higher priority. A handful of common sense and minimally invasive regulations could make all the difference for everyone on both sides of the gun control debate. Then why is it so difficult?

Powerful gun lobbying interests, political leaders, and some conservative religious groups can usually keep common-sense gun regulations from happening in any practical way. Gun safety is not a gun rights issue, but it has been made into a political and fundraising one. If you terrify people that their rights are about to be taken away, you can get them to vote and give money to causes often against their self-interest. If some leaders can keep Americans terrified and thinking from a position of fear, then no practical, logical, or fact-based discussion can be undertaken. Radicalized people cannot participate in logical discussions. That is how their leaders want them to be. Fear sells, delivering votes and lots of cash to those peddling it.

This is also an era of people spewing their hate anonymously. Anonymity makes hate so easy today. There are talkers, bullies, and cowards. Not that long ago, cowardly racist members of the KKK wore hooded masks to hide their identity when committing their crimes. The anonymity of the internet today has a similar type of mask for many people espousing racist, fascist, and anti-Semitic views. But I feel that anonymous people have nothing worth listening to. Mark Twain once said, "A mob of cowards has no sand in the presence of a man known to be splendidly brave and can easily be defeated by a single courageous person." (He used the word "sand" to describe personal courage, a common term in writing of that age.)

The day could be coming when you need to find courage. It's there inside you. So do it in public. Ahead of the Second Amendment is the First Amendment: *"Congress shall make no law respecting an establishment of religion, or prohibiting the free exercise thereof; or abridging the freedom of speech, or of the press; or the right of the people peaceably to assemble, and to petition the Government for a redress of grievances."* Americans should step up on the soapbox and state their opinion in full view of everyone else who knows exactly who they are.

Many people will criticize my comments, but Winston Churchill once said, "You will never get to your destination if you stop and throw rocks at every dog that barks at you along the way." I love that quote. Let there be critics; I don't care. Let them bark. Parotitic Americans must speak the truth in public, not from the shadows.

There is still time to protect our democracy, but you must get involved. Make sure you vote while you still can. Make certain everyone you know votes. Protest and oppose all efforts to limit or in any way impede voting or votes being counted. Keep informed and educate people about the danger of militant nationalists trying to take over our country. Don't buy into political hype from any side. Search diligently for facts that can be verified, not just read, or watch ideas that upset you without any foundation.

 Not all people who disagree with you are evil. Respect others and try to learn more about them. Even Winston Churchill, who rightly wanted to kill all Nazi nationalists during WWII, felt that the Allies should at least try to fix some of the fixable ones. Try to listen and learn from those who may not be too far gone yet. Try to find common ground with people who are not yet fascists or Nazis, but in the end, don't be foolish and fail to prepare in case all of this goes very wrong.

You might want to think of gun ownership in some of these scenarios as a safe, secure, rainy-day fund against fascists and Nazis, not a credit card for your ego, as many Americans do today.

I also have told the actual police and combat stories in this book to show you what I see and how I understand what can happen when things go wrong in tactical situations. Most things in my police career went fine, but those stories do not carry a lesson. I am alive today despite the mistakes that I and others made. Some occurred because of my errors and misjudgments. Not everything I did was a good idea at times, nor have I shared everything with you in this book. I used these stories to help you understand that making mistakes or being incautious, as I have sometimes been, can have deadly consequences for us to learn from.

Finally, you might remember the "inevitable discovery" concept described earlier in this book. It was inevitable that someday a physicist would discover that a neutron going into an unstable atom of Uranium 235 would force two neutrons out, which led to atomic bombs and, finally, the hydrogen bomb, something that could end all higher forms of life on earth. What has kept us from doing this, so far anyway, is a principle of deterrence called "Mutual Assured Destruction," or MAD for short. The idea is that no one power can use its weapons because the resulting retaliation would be so unthinkable that no one would win. Everyone would be dead at the end of the exchange. Trump supporters plan on their Civil War being successful without much fighting or bloodshed, just like Hitler as he rose to power. They know that they currently have guns, and you don't. If millions of responsible people who do not have guns today got and kept them safely, this would change the equation. They would be deterred. Their Trumpian dictatorship would come at a high cost, one they might not be willing to pay.

PART TWO

THE BORING STUFF THAT COULD SAVE YOUR LIFE

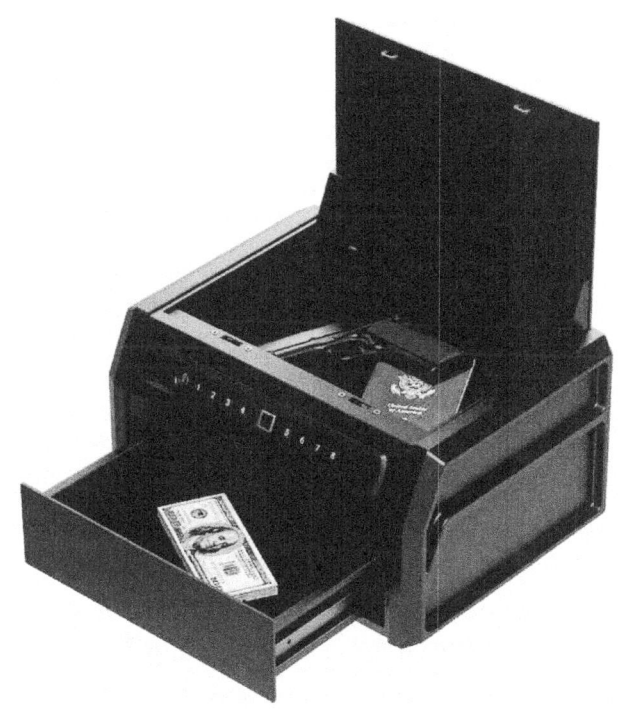

RPN3 Biometric Gun Safe with three opening systems.

CHAPTER TWENTY-ONE

FIREARM SAFETY IN YOUR HOME

Part 1 of 4 – Carrying

To get started, let's talk about keeping guns in any unsecured firearm location, including purses. Don't do it! Never leave a gun in any location that is either not on your body in a secure tamper-proof holster, in a locked safe, or at least locked with a secure trigger lock. Unfortunately, children will find handguns in their mother's purses or coat pockets and shoot someone else or themselves. It happens with unfortunate frequency. A purse or a pocket is never a safe or secure location for a firearm.

Similarly, a firearm is unsafe in a briefcase or any other package or container you carry and might lay down. A firearm you carry must always be on your person and held in a way that would make it difficult for anybody else to get it away from you. Holsters have straps, and some have locking mechanisms that make guns difficult for somebody else to seize but are accessible for the wearer to take out. Many police officers use these, and some departments require them.

If you are considering carrying a newly purchased firearm, you will need to get this security plan in place even before transporting a firearm home and make sure that everyone in your home knows the rules in advance.

Part 2 of 4– Gun Safes and Lock Boxes

One of the most important decisions you will make is how to store your gun at home safely, yet also to keep it available in case you need it to defend yourself or your family members if you are not wearing it on your person. Here are the most common choices:

Lockboxes. Firearms come from the gun shop in a simple plastic or cardboard box that is inadequate for safely storing your firearm at home. There are several ways of securing a weapon, but for starters, a locking steel gun box is one of the best. A typical handgun design is 12"x9"x4" deep and large enough for one or

RFID shotgun safe that bolts to the wall in a closet.

two handguns. It is designed to be bolted from the inside to your floor or the studs in the wall of your house. Some open with push buttons on top that must be depressed in a specific combination to open the box. Manufacturers advise you to change the combination once you get the box home, using the instructions provided because the boxes come from the factory all with the same combination.

Any locked device or safe that is easy to find is a magnet to the bad guy who might burglarize your home. It says, "Hey, important and valuable things are in here!" For that reason, keeping your locked firearm boxes out of sight is essential.

Gun Safes. The size and weight of a 600-pound gun safe will prevent it's being easily stolen or hauled off, but that is not your only consideration. Large upright gun safes, about the size of a

Opening a large free-standing gun safe quickly with a portable cutting torch.

small refrigerator, large enough to hold rifles and many other weapons, will keep people from getting their hands on a gun quickly, but they can be opened with elementary tools. I can open just about any large free-standing gun safe in about 10 minutes or less. Many criminals, even some amateurs or teenagers, can do this easily.

Using a key to open a gun safe creates a problem because anyone, even a child, knows how to use a key. If you use a safe key-operated gun, you must keep that key hidden where no one can find it. Your house or car key chain is not the correct place because your gun safe will be unsecured every time you lay down your keys.

A code-operated gun safe is a good option, but remember the sequence of numbers you have programmed into the safe and remember them quickly if you need prompt access.

Hornady Boxes. Another locking gun box is a wall-mounted security device pictured in this book. It looks like a waffle iron clamped around the center of a shotgun. Hornady makes it. You will note that it covers only part of the shotgun but keeps it from being loaded and fired when stored while also making it available to the homeowner in less than a second. This level of security is not all that far below that of a free-standing gun safe but takes up much less space and could be easily hidden. It only works properly when secured into the wall behind it with tough tempered-steel bolts and nuts.

Another feature of this gun-locking device is a Radio Frequency Identification Device, or RFID chip, to control it. It is a small square plastic piece with electronics inside that "talks" to the gun safe and, when in proximity, pops it open. You only need to move this device close to the safe to gain access to your shotgun. It takes less than a second.

Like all security devices, this safe is only as strong as its weakest part, including where it is mounted to the wall. (Please do not think your safety device is adequate if stuck through the drywall board! This may sound insultingly simplistic, but I am aware of a painful injury to a young man when exercise equipment in a commercial gym was pulled out of the drywall where it had been installed with Molly bolts that did not attach the studs behind it. Like exercise equipment, gun safes need to be installed properly.)

Biometric Safes. One of the best locking systems is a biometric safe that can be opened only with the fingerprint of an authorized person or sometimes also with a personal code that only the owner or another authorized person knows.

These work by requiring that you use your fingerprint on a small pad that you have pre-programmed into the device. You can program multiple fingerprints, usually up to 20, so you can have additional authorized people who can access the safe or use multiple fingers on your own hands in case one of your prints is too damaged or too dirty to work at any moment. Some will allow you to set a security code or use a key to open the safe. The code will allow access quickly, but the fingerprint is almost instant.

Although there are many options for sound, secure, and quick-opening safes, I will feature a few companies so you can see what they look like and how the system works for multi-opening small home gun safes. You can check many of these out online. One is called RPN3. They carry various sizes of gun safes that have all three access systems, key, biometric opening, and code. You can get the smaller ones for under $200. I have included a photo so you can see what one of them looks like. I am not endorsing that product because I have not tested it personally, but rather, I am mentioning them as a good example of what is available.

One of the biggest arguments against the safe storage of guns is that people cannot access their weapons quickly enough in an emergency. That argument does not hold water when you see how inexpensive and easy it is to have your gun available and ready to fire in only a few moments. Many finger-imprint-type biometric locks can open in a second or less. Codes can also access the safe in a second or two. There is no way you will need a gun and be able to fire it and hit anything any quicker than that. If you grab an unsecured gun and fire it in less than that time, you will either shoot someone or something that should not be shot, or you will miss it or them entirely.

Part 3 of 4 Trigger Locks

The very bare minimum of security is a good trigger lock. Because I address locks on guns or gun boxes, I have some professional training in working with locks. Some years ago, my police department sent me to attend the National Intelligence Academy in Fort Lauderdale, Florida. I took a series of classes on Basic and

Cable & key lock system for any firearm. It goes through the barrel or breech.

Advanced Lock Neutralization. I can get past most locks without too much difficulty. "Getting past" is the operative term. Although I can pick locks, I do what most criminals do and bypass the locking mechanism entirely. For example, if I wanted to steal the handgun in a locked box, I would take the whole box unless it was securely bolted to the frame of a house. Then I would open it when I got home with a torch, drill, or sledgehammer at my leisure and skip the lock. I could also reach past the locking mechanism the key goes into and manually trip the lock.

Where I can't bypass a locking mechanism, I can like plenty of bad guys, make or "impression" a key to a lock almost as fast as I can pick one. This means quickly filing a new key out of a blank one by measuring the depth of the pins in the lock. Your local hardware store usually sells locks that I can impression a key for in only a couple of minutes with some straightforward tools and a jeweler's loupe (the eyeglass-looking magnifying device they wear on their heads).

Trigger locking mechanisms of several types are useful firearm safety devices for use at home, including those immobilizing the trigger, those covering the trigger entirely, and those running a cable from the breach through the muzzle and back.

Tigger guards that immobilize the trigger reach between the trigger and the trigger guard and lock the trigger so it cannot move back and fire the gun.

Trigger guards that cover the entire trigger area are made in halves that lock together from either side of the trigger guard, securely locking the trigger into place so it cannot move. Many are accessed with keys to open them back up. You may need to look at some of the photos to see how they come apart. The biggest downside of these is storing and accessing the key itself, and sometimes a downside is the quality of the lock.

Some trigger locks attach to the loops at the end of a cable that runs either through the action or up the gun's barrel and then out the breech. This makes firearms inoperable, but only if the lock can't be easily opened and its key is hidden. The other concern with trigger locks that go through the barrel and out of the breach is the quality of the cables. Use cables such as stainless steel that cannot be easily cut. Some new guns come with them. Some are good quality, and some are not. Scrutinize them and note that locks made in America, not overseas, are generally much higher quality and more expensive.

It becomes virtually worthless if you keep the key to a trigger lock with the weapon, which many people do. If you cannot keep the keys separate, this system will not work, and no one will be any safer.

A significant debate is ongoing due to the poor quality of many trigger locks, especially ones given away by police departments and

Expanded view of the inside of a trigger lock. It goes through the trigger of any firearm. This ones uses a key to open it.

other organizations supporting greater firearms security. Online news stories and posts will show trigger locks (and safes) opened by three to six-year-olds with little difficulty. Many trigger locks can be purchased for under $4.00. A good security device to keep a child from being killed should not be the place to save money if you are planning on being a responsible gun owner.

Since 2002, the State of California has mandated that all guns sold there must have an accompanying trigger lock or locking device. Still, the state's Department of Justice Bureau of Firearms must also approve the device. You can access their safety recommendations and locking requirements here: https://oag.ca.gov/firearms. This law came into place due to the poor quality of devices that are either sold or given away.

I would also warn you against getting what are known as "disc tumbler locks," like the ones on standard filing cabinets. I can open these in no more than 2 seconds with nothing more than a paperclip. You can probably do it in less than 30 seconds without

Wheel combination trigger lock on a revolver. It fits on any firearm.

any training I have had. Teenagers and even younger kids will figure them out just as quickly.

Disc tumbler locks are easy to identify if you look inside where the key goes. There are no pins, just flat discs that slip up and down on springs. Millions of these have been made and distributed by well-meaning people and groups to get people to secure their guns. I do not believe they are safe because they are far too easy to open by anyone using minimal effort.

Trigger locks are safer if their locks have pin tumblers with at least four or five pins. Even better is a lock with at least one "mushroom" pin if you can find one. A single mushroom pin will make the lock almost unpickable. Many of them permanently jam when you pick them, so they can never be opened again after someone has tried to open them without a key. This internal self-destruct mechanism makes them among the more secure locks for any purpose. Makers of good locks will heavily advertise their safety features on the packages they are sold in.

For a little more money, you can get a biometric trigger lock. This dispenses with the key, but unlike the biometric gun safe with multiple opening mechanisms, these are usually single system opening devices. Biometric locks, although probably the most secure, also need to have a functioning power source (usually a battery or two) inside of them, and it must be a battery that has not died. They are excellent and more secure but need to be maintained, which a keyed lock does not. A good quality one costs in the range of $200.

Combination locks with little wheels and numbers on top are not a great idea. These are the ones that you see on briefcases. Once the notches on the inside edge of the wheels, which look like little gears, are all lined up, which only takes a few moments with a magnifying glass, you rotate the numbers on the top together all at once the lock pops open. The key to identifying these poor-quality locks is to look at the space between the wheels with the numbers on the top that spin and the metal on the sides. To be safe, they need to be so tight in that space that you can't see between them, even with a magnifying glass, or be able to get even a thin piece of paper down along the side. If the wheels with the numbers seem loose or wobbly, it is a worthless lock. They should fit snugly and feel almost tight when you advance the wheels with the numbers.

Lower security or cheap locking mechanisms can be opened by just reaching to the back of the lock and pulling it open, completely bypassing the entire locking system. This means that the actual mechanism that closes the lock is at the back of the lock, and a plate does not cover it. You put something small into the lock and pull it open. That takes less than one second.

Part 4 of 4 - A Crime Proof Gun - Full Biometric Firearms

I want you to know about the world's newest and potentially most secure gun. You now understand the concept of biometrics on safe gun storage; think about a gun with such a device built right into it.

You may recall that one of the biggest dangers of owning, displaying, or pointing a gun at someone is that often the bad guy will take it from you and shoot you with it. But what if someone took your gun, and it locked up inside as soon as it left your hand and could not be fired? What about a gun that could not fire a bullet by any unauthorized person in your home or anyone else?

These types of firearms are real, and more progress is being made daily. They are commonly called "smart guns." They use two different types of technology. One is the biometric system requiring your fingerprint to be wrapped around the gun handle or stock to activate the gun. Without your fingerprint, the weapon will be mechanically locked from the inside, and it cannot fire. In the past, consumers have complained that these operated too slowly. Their other problem has been with the fingerprint readers themselves. But as technology improves, so have these reading devices. The current ones are far more reliable. I think that as this technology progresses, smart firearms will become the industry standard and that someday a gun without this type of device will only be found in a museum.

The second type of "smart gun" uses a very different type of technology called RFID, or radio frequency identification device, like in the Hornady gun safe listed above. The firearm is locked from the inside until it gets into the proximity of a ring or wristwatch you are wearing. The gun and your ring or watch quickly communicate, and the gun lock automatically comes off inside the weapon. This is like a key card in a hotel or your office building. The ring or watch must be within five to ten inches for them to connect, just like a key card on a door. This way, if you drop the gun or it is taken away, it immediately locks up and cannot fire. It is improbable that a person would know that you had this device

Fingerprint biometric trigger lock that can go on any firearm. The fingerprint reader is on the side. This has a high level of safety.

or its location. However, hiding the unlocking device will become more critical if RFID weapons become familiar to the general population.

These RFID and biometric guns are not widely available in America just yet. One of the problems is that early models from American manufacturing companies misread fingerprints one out of a hundred times. These early versions were a non-starter for police departments that could not allow that malfunction rate.

The concept of smart guns has also become political. People on the right expressed anger that this technology was being developed at all, for fear it would lead to banning and seizing all guns without it. Gun rights advocates stopped buying guns from any American company considering or working on this technology. People on the left and in the technology industry themselves did not want to make anything that helped more people acquire guns, no matter how safe they were. They were both wrong.

Wherever there is a market, entrepreneurs will emerge to provide any product that people will buy. This marketplace will be evolving in new ways after January 6, 2021. Any gunmaker not offering these soon will be on the outside looking in on a very lucrative market. Some European companies are perfecting this technology and continuing where their American counterparts left off only a few years ago.

One American company developing these biometric firearms is called Biofire. They launched a new website in 2021. Although I am not endorsing or recommending their specific product because I have not personally tested it yet, you can read more about the firm online and even be put on a list for when their products become available. As a consumer, you can influence the future marketplace by supporting these more innovative products over less-safe firearms.

No new safety technology is ever perfect at first, but a long time ago, people said the same thing about seat belts and, later, airbags in cars. Today, we would not think of driving a car without both. In the not-too-distant future, every vehicle in the world will have a backup camera, just so we don't run over little kids on bikes and pedestrians. The same will be true of technology for smart guns.

CHAPTER TWENTY-TWO

PERSONAL FIREARM SAFETY

Knowing some basic rules on firearm safety is essential. Understand them before you buy one and bring it home. Getting a copy of an owner's manual and reading it beforehand is easy. You can almost always get one online for your new gun purchase. Heed all warnings, of which there will be many. Gun manufacturers want you to have this information on the weapon you buy.

Here is a typical generic warning for a firearm that you can find online (this approximates the format of many warnings):

Read the instructions and warnings in this manual BEFORE any use of this firearm.
WARNING
READ THESE INSTRUCTIONS AND WARNINGS WITH SERIOUS CAUTION. BE SURE YOU UNDERSTAND THESE INSTRUCTIONS AND WARNINGS BEFORE USING THIS

GUN GUIDE FOR DEMOCRATS

FIREARM IN ANY WAY. FAILURE TO READ THESE INSTRUCTIONS AND TO FOLLOW THESE WARNINGS MAY RESULT IN SERIOUS INJURY OR DEATH TO YOU AND OTHERS OR DAMAGE TO PROPERTY.
This SAFETY & INSTRUCTION MANUAL should always accompany any firearm and be transferred with it upon change of ownership or when presented to another person for their use of the weapon. A copy of the SAFETY & INSTRUCTION MANUAL is available FREE via download at www.[manufacturers website].com or upon request from:
[gun manufacturers name] CUSTOMER SUPPORT CENTER & Company address
TEL.: 1-800-555-5555, ext. 5555 E-mail: email address
YOUR SAFETY & RESPONSIBILITIES
SAFETY IS YOUR RESPONSIBILITY
At home, in the field, at the range, or anywhere, the first concern of every firearm owner should be safety. Apply the following safety rules in every situation, with any kind of firearm. If you feel uncertain about any operational aspects of your firearm, please contact [the gun manufacturer's name and phone number are usually here] before proceeding with its operation. If you are unfamiliar with firearms, you should seek formal training before using your revolver.
WARNING: YOU MUST FOLLOW ALL OF THESE SAFETY RULES TO ENSURE THE SAFE USE OF THIS OR ANY FIREARM.
THE FAILURE TO FOLLOW THE INSTRUCTIONS AND WARNINGS IN THIS MANUAL COULD CAUSE SERIOUS PERSONAL INJURY OR DEATH TO YOU

**OR OTHERS AND DAMAGE TO PROPERTY.
As a firearm owner, you accept a serious responsibility. How seriously you take this responsibility can be the difference between life and death. There is no excuse for careless or abusive handling of your firearm. At all times handle your firearm with intense respect for its power and potential danger to you and others.**

There are usually triangle warnings of all kinds to catch your attention. And exclamation points throughout!!! Some of this is in bright colors, just so you pay attention and take this all seriously. The manuals usually include the maker's phone number, mailing address, and email, just in case something is not clear. Here are the key basic rules that you need to know and obey:

1. ALWAYS KEEP YOUR FIREARM POINTED IN A SAFE DIRECTION. Don't point a firearm at anyone or anything you do not intend to shoot and kill, whether it is loaded or not. This is particularly important when loading, unloading or disassembling the gun. ALWAYS control the direction of the firearm in all conditions no matter where you are.

2. ALWAYS TREAT EVERY FIREARM AS IF IT IS LOADED AND WILL FIRE. Do not take anyone's word that the firearm is unloaded – always check for yourself. Never pass your firearm to another person until the cylinder or action is open and you visually check yourself that it is unloaded. Keep your firearm unloaded and safely stored when not in use. (There will be debate about quick access to a firearm for self-defense at home, but this is the general rule)

3. NEVER PLACE YOUR FINGER INSIDE THE TRIGGER GUARD OR ON THE TRIGGER UNLESS YOU INTEND TO FIRE. Ensure that no other objects can reach inside the trigger-guard or can touch the trigger because they could snag and pull the trigger.

4. ALWAYS BE SURE OF YOUR TARGET AND WHAT IS BEYOND IT. Always be sure of where any bullet can possibly strike and shoot only where there is a safe backstop free of obstructions, water, or other surfaces which can cause ricochets. Be sure your bullet will stop behind your target without going through. Bullets can glance off many hard surfaces like rocks. Be aware that bullets can ricochet off the surface of water and travel in unpredictable directions with considerable velocity. Never fire randomly into the sky.

5. NEVER CROSS OBSTACLES SUCH AS FENCES OR STREAMS WITH A LOADED FIREARM. Always make certain your firearm is unloaded before crossing a fence, climbing a tree, jumping a ditch, or negotiating any type of obstacle of any kind where you cannot fully and completely control your firearm. The trigger could get snagged and fire the weapon.

6. SAFE GUN HANDLING IS YOUR RESPONSIBILITY AT ALL TIMES. Firearms are dangerous and can cause serious injury or death if they are misused or used inappropriately. Safety must be the prime consideration of anyone who owns or handles firearms. Accidents are the result of violating the rules of safe gun handling and common sense. Firearm safety training is available and necessary. Contact your firearms

dealer, law enforcement agency, local sportsman's club, etc. for availability.

7. YOU ARE RESPONSIBLE FOR THE FIREARM AT ALL TIMES. In owning a firearm, you must undertake full-time responsibility for your firearm's safety and security. You must protect yourself and all others against injury or death from misuse of the firearm 24 hours a day.

8. FIREARM SECURITY IS YOUR RESPONSIBILITY. You must secure firearms safely from children and unauthorized users. Your firearm should always be kept unloaded and locked when not in use. (Again, some argue for quicker access, but this is a basic rule) A lock is sometimes provided with your firearm for this purpose. Never assume that the use of this lock is sufficient to safely secure your firearm. Check the quality of the locking device yourself. You must always evaluate your situation and employ the security systems that meet your needs and prevents children and unauthorized users from gaining access to your firearm. Do not assume that the lock that comes with a gun is fully adequate and do your research. See Chapter 16, Firearm Safety in Your Home.

9. APPROPRIATE USE FOR YOUR FIREARM MEANS USING YOUR FIREARM FOR LEGAL PURPOSES. Use your firearm for target shooting, hunting, and _lawful_ resistance of deadly crime in progress in your home. It is your responsibility to ensure that you are following all applicable laws and ordinances regarding the use of your firearm. To aim your firearm at another person without legal justification to do so is the crime of assault.

10. NEVER RELY ON MECHANICAL SAFETY FEATURES ALONE. Only your safe gun-handling habits will ensure the safe use of your firearm. This is your responsibility. Don't rely on the internal mechanical safety of the gun as your only security device.

11. ALWAYS SAFELY STORE AND SECURE YOUR FIREARM. Safe and secure storage of your firearm is one of your most important responsibilities. It is a full-time responsibility. See Chapter 16, "Firearm Safety in Your Home."

12. NEVER KEEP AMMUNITION IN THE SAME LOCATION AS THE FIREARM. Store each in a separate and secure place. (This is a basic rule, a good starting place.). See Chapter 16 on Firearms Safety at Home and Chapter 21, "What to Hide and Where to Hide It."

13. ALWAYS WEAR EYE PROTECTION THAT IS SPECIFIED FOR USE WITH FIREARMS. Wear eye protection every time you handle your firearm for target practice, cleaning, and maintenance. A billed baseball cap also can help protect you from being hit by hot brass being ejected from your firearm after you fire it.

14. ALWAYS WEAR EAR PROTECTORS THAT ARE SPECIFIED FOR USE WITH FIREARMS. Use ear protection every time you discharge your firearm. Make sure that others in the vicinity of where you will be shooting do so as well. That includes other users at the range.

15. NEVER USE ALCOHOL OR DRUGS BEFORE OR WHILE SHOOTING. Do not use your firearm if you are on any

prescription or over-the-counter medication that could impair your mental state or reflexes, or any alcohol of any kind, which impairs, even slightly, your mental or physical ability. Not even one sip of alcohol is okay. Don't have it close by when using firearms.

16. ALWAYS HAVE ADEQUATE VENTILATION. Discharging firearms in poorly ventilated areas, cleaning firearms, or handling ammunition may result in exposure to lead and other substances that are known to cause birth defects, reproductive harm, and other serious physical injuries. Review the warnings and labels for all ammunition and cleaning products carefully. Wash hands and clothes thoroughly after exposure.

17. BEFORE HANDLING ANY FIREARM, UNDERSTAND ITS OPERATION. Not all firearms operate the same. Familiarize yourself with the mechanical features of any firearm you intend to use. If you feel uncertain about any operational aspects of your firearm, please contact the manufacturer before its use or get professional training by a qualified trainer.

18. NEVER ALLOW A FIREARM TO BE USED BY INDIVIDUALS WHO DO NOT UNDERSTAND ITS SAFE OPERATION OR HAVE NOT READ THESE FIREARM SAFETY RULES OR FAIL TO AGREE TO OBEY THE RULES.

19. ALWAYS USE THE CORRECT AMMUNITION FOR YOUR PARTICULAR FIREARM as indicated by the marking on the barrel. Never use non-standard, reloaded, or "hand-loaded" ammunition that has not been subjected to internal

ballistic pressure testing. Only use reloaded or non-factory hand-loaded ammunition after proper training and research. Do not use ammunition that someone gives to you without proper knowledge about it.

20. BEWARE OF BARREL OBSTRUCTIONS Be sure the barrel is clear of obstructions before shooting. Mud, water, snow, or other objects may inadvertently lodge in the barrel. A small obstruction can cause a dangerous increase in pressure inside the firearm and may damage your gun and cause injury to yourself and others when it is fired.

21. BE SURE ALL ACCESSORIES, SUCH AS HOLSTERS, GRIPS, SLINGS, SCOPES, AND OTHER ACCESSORIES ARE COMPATIBLE with the firearm and that the accessories do not interfere with its safe operation. It is your responsibility to understand and follow all the instructions in the manual for your gun, well as those which may be supplied with your ammunition and any accessory.

22. NEVER DISASSEMBLE YOUR FIREARM beyond the simple disassembly procedures outlined in the manual. Improper disassembly or reassembly of your firearm may be dangerous and can lead to serious injury or death.

23. NEVER MANIPULATE, ADJUST OR CHANGE ANY OF THE INTERNAL COMPONENTS OF YOUR FIREARM UNLESS SPECIFICALLY INSTRUCTED TO DO SO IN YOUR MANUAL. Improper manipulation of any other internal component may affect the safety and reliability of your firearm and may cause serious injury or death. Never accept any advice from people on the internet. Get your

information only from qualified experts recognized by manufacturers or from reliable licensed and insured gunsmiths.

24. NEVER ALLOW ANY ALTERATION OR REPLACEMENT OF PARTS IN YOUR FIREARM UNLESS PERFORMED BY A QUALIFIED GUNSMITH using genuine parts. If you do otherwise, improper functioning of your firearm may occur, and serious injury or death and property damage may result.

Those are just some of the basics when it comes to firearms handling. I would call them the 24 basic commandments of gun ownership.

There are other considerations that a person needs to know before even opening the box that their firearm comes in or transporting it home. State laws vary as to whether a firearm in the cab of your vehicle must be on your body or can be on the seat or under the seat next to you or whether it must be locked in the trunk. You can learn the details by reading state statutes and local ordinances or often by asking your local dealer or professional trainer.

A friend's story exemplifies how seriously you should follow firearm safety rules. She grew up in a family that hunted, and she participated as a member of a target shooting team during her four years of high school. At home, she could not aim even a squirt gun at another person. She raised her sons never to point a TV remote controller at someone because it might be mistaken for a gun.

I saw one person with a TV remote controller in his hand shot by police and another person in a hallway during a search warrant who was missed by only inches when the detective mistook his TV remote controller for a gun. The police bullet hit a wall clock just behind the person. Fortunately, the person was not injured, but the detective was kidded for years for "killing time."

If you know a firearm and its operation, you must understand how to clean it and keep it operating correctly. Whenever you fire a weapon, it combusts explosive materials and releases hot, expanding gasses. Metals are being forced down the gun's bore, scoring and leaving deposits in the barrel. If you have ever seen a slow-motion video of a gun being fired, you can see all this material burning and coming out the barrel, the breach, and even the trigger area of the gun. That leaves a residue that needs to be cleaned up on the inside and outside of the gun. Build-up can damage the weapon and cause the firearm to malfunction, causing you or others to be injured or killed. Even if you fire a gun just once, it needs to be cleaned appropriately, then correctly stored.

Cleaning many firearms is easy, but you need the proper tools—the more complex the firearm, the more work it takes to clean it. Ensure you have read the manual and do not take a gun out to a range or the woods before ensuring it is clean and safe. Each firearm will have specific cleaning requirements.

This book does not address any firearm's loading, unloading, and maintenance. They are all different from gun to gun; you need the correct information for the gun you buy or store.

Suppose you have questions about any of these processes or a specific weapon. In that case, there is likely a professional gunsmith in your area that can supply information or even assess the condition of a used weapon.

It is illegal to shoot at trees or use them to hold targets. These trees on public land have been shot down with fully-automatic military assault-style weapons.

CHAPTER TWENTY-THREE

RANGE SAFETY

The basic rules of personal firearm safety always apply, and there are a few others you will need to know if you will shoot at a target range. Rules for a specific indoor or outdoor range will almost always be prominently posted so everyone can see and read them. Some outdoor locations other than ranges allow recreational shooting, and there will be rules for this activity. Often, these will not be posted, but you must know and follow them. Here are some of the basic rules from the United States Forest Service for shooting on its public lands:

Target shooting is allowed on national forests or grassland unless restricted. Check your local ranger district for more information about local restrictions. It is prohibited to shoot:

1. In or within 150 yards from a residence, building, campsite, developed recreation area, or occupied area. (*Editorial Note from the Author: Personally, I think that this is nuts and it should be much further away from any of these activities or locations. Shooting near anyone camping is not only very disrespectful but will eventually get all shooting in public places banned.*)
2. Across or on a national forest or grassland road or body of water.
3. In any manner or place where any person or property is exposed to injury or damage because of such discharge.
   — Into or within a cave.
   — Firing tracer bullets or incendiary ammunition.
   — Disturbing, injuring, destroying, or in any way damaging any prehistoric, historic, or archaeological resource, structure, site, artifact, property.
   — Abandoning any personal property or failing to dispose of all garbage, including targets, paper, cans, bottles, appliances.
   — Use approved targets. Certain forests may have specific restrictions, such as the type of targets used (i.e., cardboard targets, paper targets, clay pigeons). Exploding targets are not recommended and are restricted on many forests or grasslands for safety and fire concerns. [They are also illegal in many states and actually are illegal on most other public lands]

— Use approved targets along with a safe," bullet-proof" backstop. Do not attach your targets to vegetation or structures, such as trees, log decks, slash piles, fences, or water tanks.
- Practice safe gun handling by:
  - Treating every gun as if it is loaded.
  - Never let the muzzle of a firearm point at anything you do not intend to shoot.
  - Keep your finger off the trigger until your sights are on the target and you are ready to shoot.
  - Make sure of your target and what is beyond.
  - Do not have alcoholic beverages while discharging a firearm."

These are the basics, but they are only a starting place for you to do more research on your own, either with the gun manufacturer or online from reliable and reputable sources, like Federal, state, and local government websites. Stay away from blogs or other online nonsense that is often politically biased and ignores science and common-sense facts. It is unfortunate, but people can learn bad habits from seeing what other people post online on places like YouTube.

It will be up to you to abide by safety rules in the woods and on open rangeland. If wooded or public-looking areas are not public property but rather owned by private companies or individuals, I can guarantee you that all shooting on these lands is trespass and illegal. Please do not do it. Respect private land rights. Some private owners will allow hunting, but they usually ask that you get permission before hunting or shooting there. They'll inform you of their rules ahead of time, usually in writing, and require a written permit.

Person with a .50 caliber sniper rifle with a scope in the forest on public land.

Finally, try your level best to understand your moral and social responsibility to reduce conflicts with other users of forests and public lands. Be respectful, courteous, and kind when using public lands for target shooting. More of them are being closed all the time because of illegal, disrespectful, or destructive behavior. There is room for everyone if people would do more to adopt this concept. Positively interact with those who are not doing so. Try to find respectful common ground.

Illegal, toxic and exploding targets from USFS lands.

CHAPTER TWENTY-FOUR

~

FIRING WILD - GUNS IN THE FOREST

As you plan to acquire and train with your firearm, you may be tempted to skip the range and go to the woods to fire your gun. Please do not do that. Heading to the woods to begin banging away is like attending medical school right after kindergarten. Looking for public places to shoot should only come after competent firearms training from an instructor.

There may be a place to shoot or train later once you are properly acquainted with your firearm. The basic range safety rules and all those standards also apply to the woods or public lands. Public lands will also have individual local standards and rules about where you can shoot and what you can shoot into or around.

If you go open shooting in these places, consider this: Many areas are destroyed by irresponsible shooters. This is unfortunate because, appropriately done, target shooting can be a compatible use of public lands. The explosion of gun sales in the last ten years has led to a staggering misuse of our public lands by unintelligent, drunk, unsafe, and uninformed gun owners. Millions of dollars of damage in the form of wildfires and pollution have been caused in Washington State by illegal and hazardous target shooting.

I live close to one of those areas near a national forest and always see it. One shooting area that is now closed saw eight wildfires in a single summer from users shooting illegal explosive targets. One happened in August when the temperature was 87 degrees with only 17% humidity, making fire danger very high. Citizens in my area formed a group to inform shooters, clean up the mess, and get some dangerous places closed. The Washington State legislative staff made a public video that shows what it looks like in the forests when these nitwits come up with their weapons. I would suggest you look at it now. It can be found here on YouTube – it's called Firing Wild:

https://www.youtube.com/watch?v=sNMBCQowVjM

The stupid stuff you will see here was posted by the idiots themselves online. You can't make this stuff up. I want you to remember two things. The first is that these people know nothing about firearms or firearm safety. You need to watch out for and stay away from them in the woods. The second is another point I am trying to make in this book about the actual danger from most Americans with firearms today. You will note the lack of discipline and thought many have put into owning firearms. These are not tactically disciplined people. Some are not even very bright. Many such American gun owners pose as significant a risk to themselves as to others.

Some of the idiots using these areas were bringing up cars, cranking the steering wheels into a turn with the seatbelt, putting a brick on the accelerator, and then jumping out. The vehicle would spin wildly out of control in circles at high speed with no one in it. They would blast away with AR-15-type weapons until the car exploded into flames; they'd keep shooting until the car finally stopped with thousands of bullets and holes in it. Shooting cars, electronics, and giant TVs leave toxic chemicals.

Another subject to think about when target training in the woods or on public lands open to shooting is the dual problem of toxic chemicals and lead. Each causes a toxic risk.

Stupid people with guns learn which chemicals make enormous fireballs and bring those materials up to the woods. Unfortunately, many of these chemicals that look so cool when they blow up are also carcinogenic, and the heavy metals in them are persistent in the environment.

One area near where I live had so much shooting of toxic chemicals that we hired a lab to analyze the soil. It showed significant levels of dangerous toxic chemicals that could contaminate a person just by walking in the area. We presented the results to the USFS, and the area was closed to shooting and capped and sealed with a deep overlay of gravel at significant expense to the taxpayers.

The second problem was the levels of lead in this area. One area had lead levels 1,800 times above what is considered toxic in

Exploding targets like this Tanerite by Sonic Boom are illegal on most public lands and start forest fires.

a workplace environment. It would have qualified as a superfund site.

If you shoot in the woods, you can expect lead levels to be this high if the area has been used for some time. No one cleans up the lead like they often do at a shooting range where they have a safety feature called lead traps. This does not mean you cannot shoot there, but you must know that your shoes can be contaminated until you clean them. If I am walking in these areas, I use a separate set of shoes that I keep in a sealed package in the trunk of my car. I slip them on and off from the driver's seat from a short distance away from the firing range and then put a plastic garbage bag on the floor of my car to keep my vehicle uncontaminated. When I change back into my clean shoes, I drop the dirty shoes into the contaminated bag without touching the outside, keeping my trunk clean.

It would be best if you never ate or drank anything in an active shooting area like this, or any other location for that matter, where guns have been fired. This is a warning that most gun manufacturers will advise you of when you purchase a firearm. It would be best to never touch your mouth or face after shooting, handling a gun, or even being in this area because you can ingest lead. Enough lead in your system, or more seriously, in the system of a younger person, can cause cancer and brain damage. Hostility, agitation, anger, paranoia, and insanity can result from ingesting lead.

You will also see many people with military assault-style weapons in the woods. The reason is that many ranges don't allow them to be shot on their property. Additionally, there is no range master on public lands to control their behavior like on most gun ranges. You must keep an eye out for these people and keep your distance. Many are abjectly unsafe in basic firearms handling.

The good news is that you can help prevent this from happening. You can also help protect our public lands from irresponsible shooters by reporting bad actors. Although it may not be your cup of tea, I ask them to stop if I see someone shooting illegally. They usually only do it because no one ever asks them to stop, and in some cases, they do not know the rules. I will tell them where they can shoot legally and what legal and safe targets are. The vast majority are polite and not confrontational. Some thank me for the information.

We are all in this together regarding protecting our public lands. Our group has substantially reduced illegal and unsafe target shootings and trash in my area in the last six years. Our group is called the White River Forest Protection Association, with shooters and non-shooters among our members.

CHAPTER TWENTY-FIVE

A VISUAL BASIC SUMMARY OF FIREARMS & TERMS

If you are unfamiliar with basic firearms terms, I include this chapter so you can understand the ones you might need to make sense of in the earlier chapters. Many terms will make more sense when you look at the corresponding photographs showing some of them. If you are familiar with these terms, skip to the other chapter.

Action - the mechanism that fires a gun:

>Single Action firearm - You must pull a hammer back and lock it in place to cock it prior to pulling the trigger to fire the weapon.

>Double Action firearm– When you pull the trigger, the hammer comes back then drops the firing pin onto the bullet to fire the weapon in one motion, but you can pull the hammer

GUN GUIDE FOR DEMOCRATS

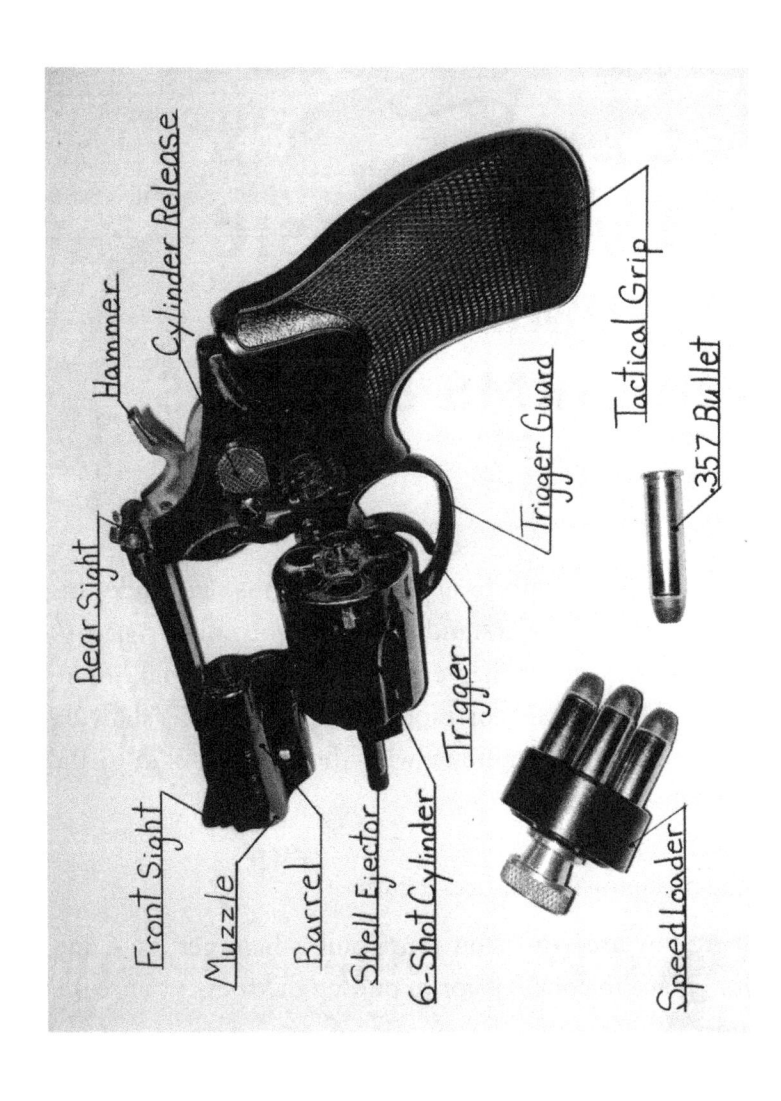

Parts of a double-action six-shot revolver with a speed loader, in this case a Smith & Wesson Model 19 .357 Magnum that can also fire .38 Special rounds.

back and lock it into place manually, prior to pulling the trigger, if you prefer.

Semi-Automatic –When you pull the trigger, the firearm loads a bullet in the chamber, pulls the hammer back, fires, and reloads the next bullet automatically, but it only shoots one bullet for each pull of the trigger. Some of these weapons have no visible hammer on the outside. If there is not a round in the chamber when you begin, you must pull on a lever at the side of the gun by the chamber to manually put the first round or shell in place to begin the process. This also cocks the gun for the first shot.

Fully-Automatic – Same as the semi-automatic, but the gun keeps firing with a single pull until all the bullets have been fired from the gun. Usually, these fire around eight bullets per second until they are gone. These seldom have a visible hammer on the outside.

Ammunition: People tend to use the terms "bullet," "cartridge," "shell," "rounds" and "case" interchangeably. This section will explain the difference between those terms.

Shell or Cartridge – The cylindrical container that holds the gunpowder, lead tip of the bullet, and primer. They are usually made of brass, but they can be made of steel, aluminum, plastic, or in the case of shotgun shells, paper.

Bullet – Projectile that is fired from a gun, usually made of lead, sometimes covered by copper, but can be steel. The lead tip of a cartridge that is expelled from a shell when a firearm is fired. Commonly, the entire cartridge and lead are called a bullet.

GUN GUIDE FOR DEMOCRATS

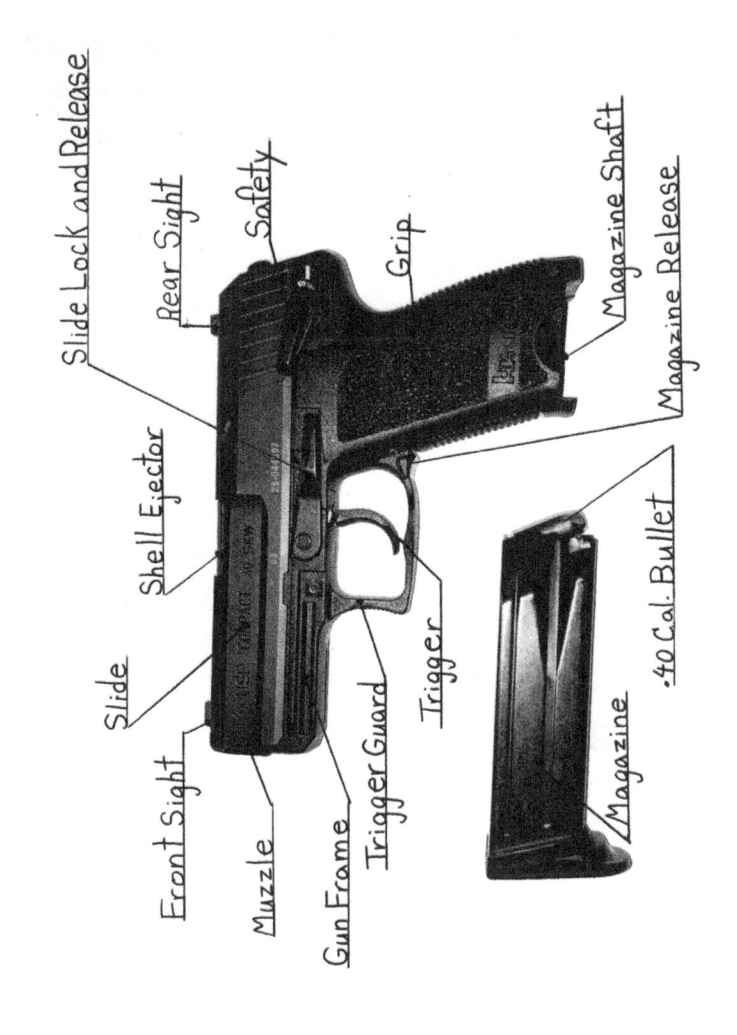

Parts of a semi-automatic hand gun, in this case a H&K that fires a .40 cal Smith & Wesson round.

Primer--The chemical contact explosive that sparks when struck by a firing pin, igniting the gunpowder in a cartridge.

Centerfire – Bullets that have primer at the back of the shell, in the center, which is hit by the firing pin after being released by the hammer.

Rimfire – Bullets that have their primer material at the back of the shell just inside of the rim, so the firing pin hits the shell on the edge, instead of in the center.

Shotgun Rounds or Shells – A round means a shell or case. Shotgun ammunition is usually called a shell and handgun and rifle ammunition are usually called rounds.

Powder, Gunpowder – The compound that explodes in the shell so that expanding pressure forces the bullet out of the muzzle of the firearm. Different types burn or explode at different speeds. Handgun powder usually explodes much faster than rifle powder because they have shorter barrels.

Black Powder – The original gunpower that explodes and does not burn. It is much more unstable than modern gunpower and even static electricity can set it off.

Birdshot – Shotgun pellets that are small and are usually used for hunting birds.

Buckshot – Large shotgun pellets that are usually used for killing people or large game. Often there are nine .17 caliber pellets in a shell.

Aught (written as "0") – The size of some shotgun pellets.

Target Ammunition – Ammunition and bullets for shooting paper targets at a range. They are generally inexpensive and of poor quality. These often include lead slugs without copper covering or jackets.

Jacketed Bullets – Bullets that have a copper covering not extending over the lead tip.

Full Metal Jacket & Military (NATO) ammunition – This is generally military ammunition that complies with the North Atlantic Treaty Organization and Hauge Conventions prohibiting bullets that expand or cause too much damage when they hit a person. The copper covering covers the entire bullet.

Hollowpoint – Bullets that have a hole in the lead slug at the tip, so they expand when hitting an object.

Dum Dum – An older term for a bullet that is soft on the end and expands when it hits something, usually a person.

Slug – A large piece of lead that is fired out of a shotgun as a single piece as opposed to smaller lead or steel pellets.

Assault Weapon, Assault-style weapon – A broad term usually referring to a semi-automatic or fully-automatic firearm with a detachable magazine, a pistol grip, and sometimes other features such as a vertical forward grip (handle under the barrel), flash suppressor, or barrel shroud. Certain firearms are specified by name in some laws that restrict assault weapons in different jurisdictions. When the now-defunct Federal Assault Weapons Ban was passed in 1994, the U.S. Department of Justice said, "In general, assault weapons are semiautomatic firearms with a large magazine of ammunition designed and configured for rapid fire and combat use." Still, the commonly used definitions of assault weapons are under frequent debate and change all the time. Honestly, this term does not mean much anymore, as so many different firearms might qualify these days. In common terms, it means what any

A VISUAL BASIC SUMMARY OF FIREARMS & TERMS   199

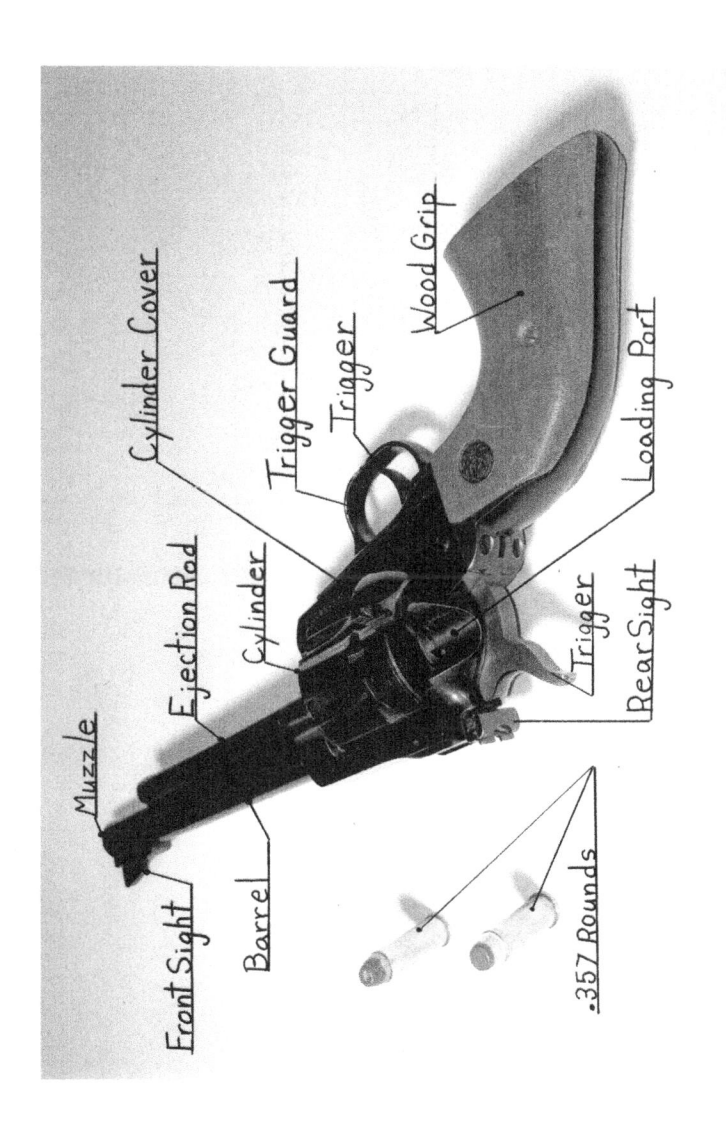

Parts of a single-action six-shot revolver, in this case a Ruger .357 Magnum that also can fire .38 Special rounds.

GUN GUIDE FOR DEMOCRATS

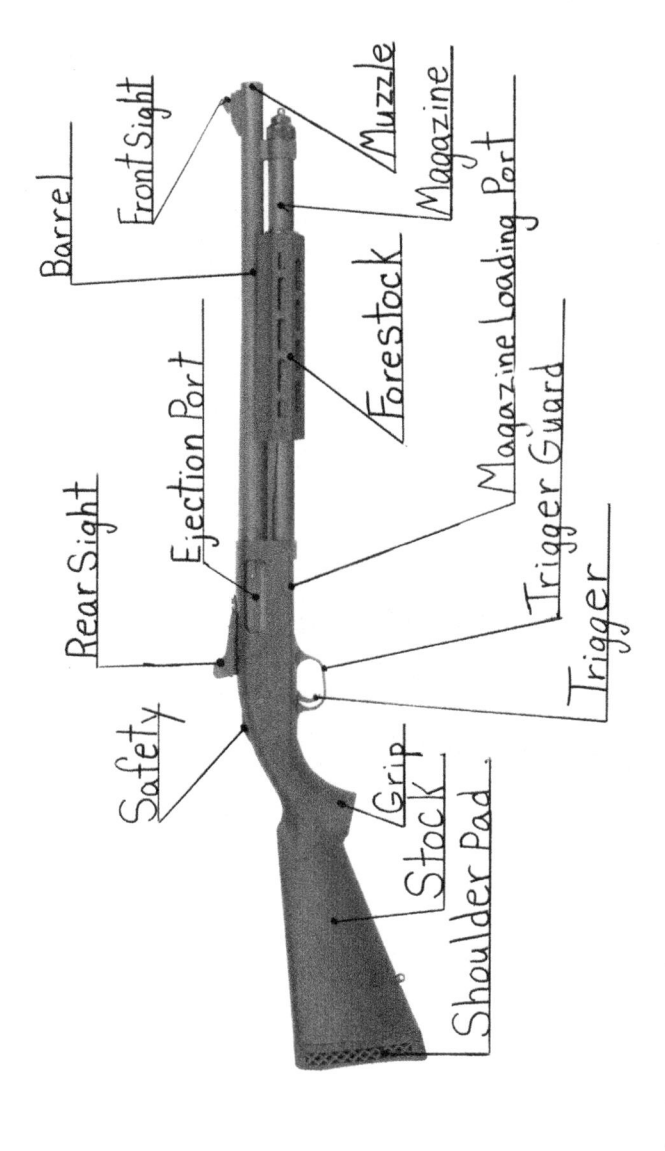

Parts of a shotgun, in this case a Mossberg 590A1 Tactical pump-action model.

particular person thinks it means, based on their vision of a military weapon of war.

Barrel - The tube of a firearm from which the bullet is expelled. The hole through the barrel is the bore.

Rifling: Grooves machined in a spiral into the inside of a bore that makes a fired bullet spin as it travels down the barrel.

Smooth Bore – A barrel with no rifling in the barrel. Few modern firearms (rifles and handguns) are made this way, but all shotguns have smooth bores.

Caliber - The size of the ammunition that a weapon is designed to shoot, as measured by the bullet's approximate diameter in inches in the United States, and in millimeters in other countries. In some instances, ammunition is described with additional terms, such as the year of its introduction (30/06) or the name of the designer (.30 Newton). In some countries, ammunition is also described in terms of the length of the cartridge case (7.62 x 63 mm).

Carbine – A short barrel rifle, often a military one.

Chamber, or Breach – The place where the entire bullet case or shell goes in a firearm so that it is in position to be fired when hit by the hammer; the position in the action that the bullet is fired from.

Cylinder – A round metal piece that holds the shells or bullets for a revolver, usually a handgun.

Firing Pin – A metal part of the hammer that hits a bullet, igniting the primer and setting off the explosion in the case or shell.

Gauge, as in 12-Gauge - Shotguns are classified by gauge, which is a measure related to the diameter of the smooth shotgun bore and the size of the shotshell designed for that bore. Common

GUN GUIDE FOR DEMOCRATS

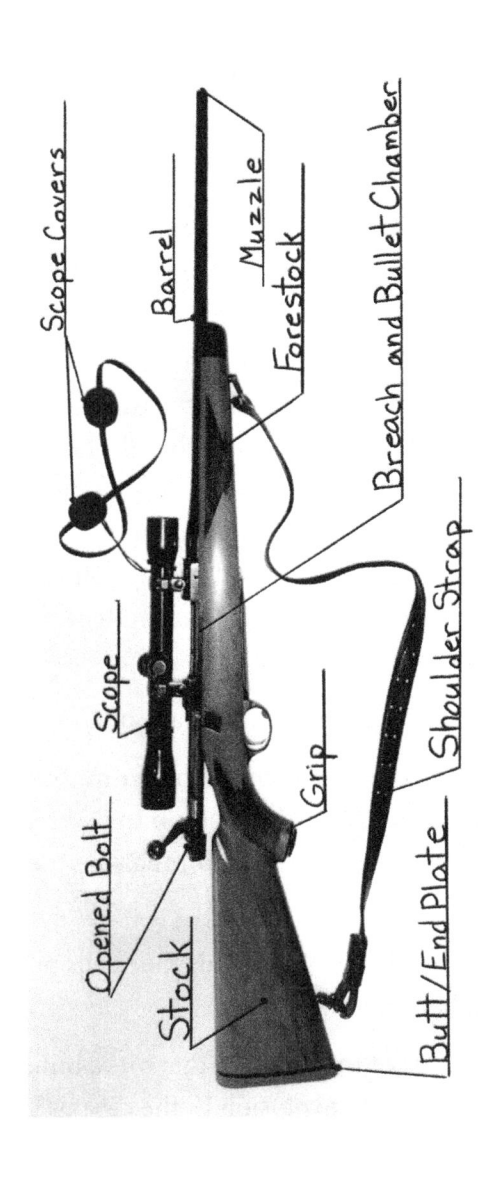

Parts of a typical single-shot bolt-action rifle with a scope, scope covers, and shoulder strap, in this case a Ruger .270 Winchester.

shotgun gauges are 10-gauge, 12-gauge, 16-gauge, 20-gauge, and 410-gauge. The smaller the gauge number, the larger the shotgun bore.

Hammer – The part of the action that is released by the trigger to cause the firing pin to hit the bullet to fire a firearm. It is spring-loaded. It moves with a significant force to drive the firing pin onto the bullet to cause it to explode.

Hang-fire – You fire the weapon, but the powder fails to fully ignite or there is a light charge of powder, and the bullet only travels a short distance down the barrel and stops and is jammed there. If a second round is fired, it can blow up the gun and seriously injure or kill the person firing the weapon. This danger is far greater with automatic weapons.

Magazine – The container for bullets in a firearm. This piece is either built into the firearm itself or is a separate piece, or clip, which is slipped into the firearm, usually at the bottom below the chamber.

Magnum – Just a made-up term to make a firearm seem more powerful than it looks or is. Its actual meaning is a bottle of wine that is twice the size of a normal one. A trade name.

Misfire – You pull the trigger, and the hammer comes down on the primer, but it fails to fire.

Musket – A smooth bore firearm, usually a long-barreled one. These were once common but are now rare.

Pistol – A small gun you can hold in your hand.

Revolver – A handgun that holds multiple bullets, usually five or six, in a round cylinder that rotates after each time you fire, moving the next bullet into position to be fired.

GUN GUIDE FOR DEMOCRATS

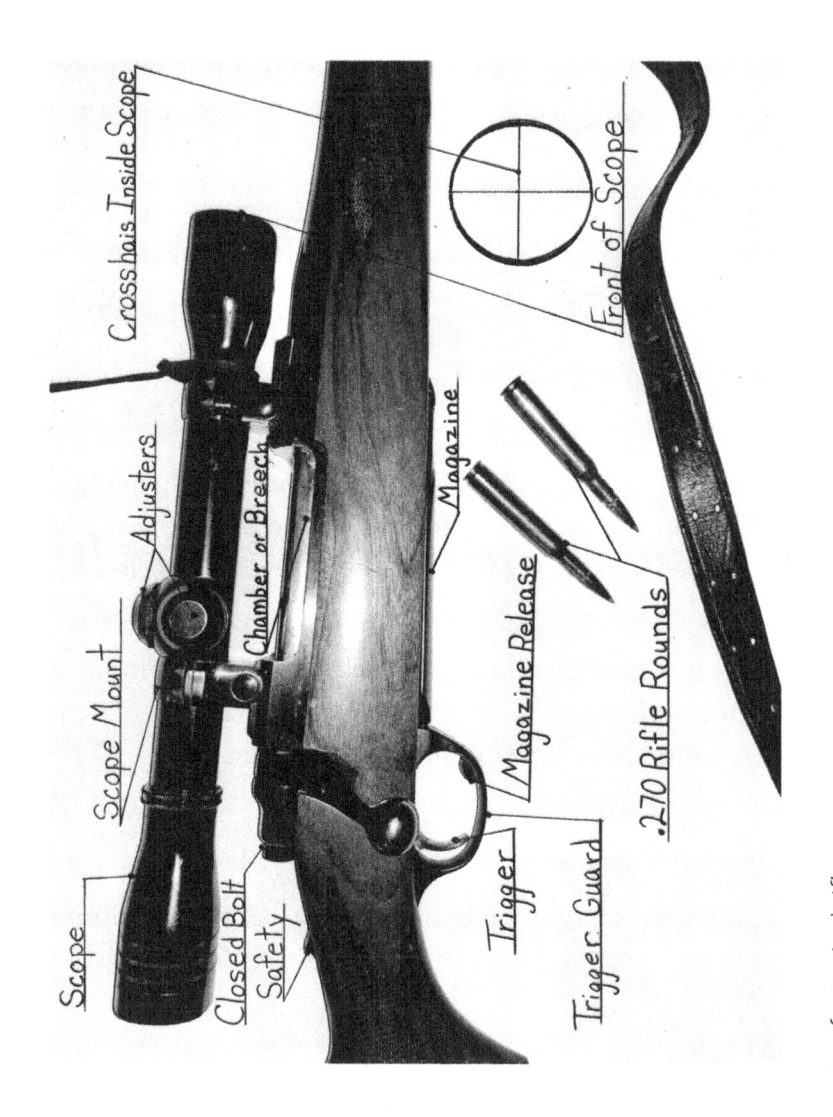

Additional parts of a typical rifle.

Rifle as opposed to Rifling – A rifle is a long gun designed to be shot from the shoulder, as opposed to a shorter handgun shot from the hand. Most people today call all long firearms except shotguns rifles, even if they do not have rifling cut into the barrel.

Sighting In – To adjust the mechanical or optical scope on any firearm to assure that the scope is synchronized with the barrel, so the firearm is correctly aimed at the image visible in the scope.

Special, as in .38 Special – Just another made-up word that infers something better than just a .38 caliber round of ammunition. A trade name.

Tactical – An encounter with another person, usually with firearms or a weapon, where the outcome has the risk of injury or death.

Trigger – The lever on the outside at the bottom of a firearm that you pull to fire the gun.

CHAPTER TWENTY-SIX

BULLET DETAILS

Weapons today fire stable gunpowder that does not explode, even if you throw a match into it. It just burns. Most modern gunpowder can explode only if it is contained in a confined space.

The typical ignition source for modern firearms is a "primer," a stable chemical like mercury fulminate, a contact explosive. The brass or silver-colored cartridge with the pointed lead bullet on the end is called the "shell" or "case" containing the gunpowder. When the trigger is pulled, the gun's hammer strikes the primer with a firing pin, and the primer explodes, igniting the gunpowder, which also explodes, propelling the bullet out the end of the barrel.

Some high-velocity bullets generating such great shock and force are no good for hunting. Animals shot with too high of velocity rounds will suffer so much damage as to be "blood-shot," and as much as a quarter of the animal is useless as food because the bullet's energy destroys it. Responsible hunters understand this and do not use such rounds.

Some rounds, like the Wetherbee .300 Magnum or .458 Winchester Magnum, were developed for killing elephants or other large African animals. Some hunters still use them for smaller North American game and most animals shot with them can be destroyed on impact due to this shock factor. This is wasteful and foolish.

The longer the barrel, the more time the bullet gains speed before leaving the muzzle. Generally, handgun rounds travel slower than rifle rounds because the barrel is shorter, but the larger caliber ones still go fast enough to do substantial damage.

One last note is on steel ammunition for rifles or handguns. It is inexpensive. It's also common for people with military assault-style weapons, especially fully automatic ones, to buy and use because they fire so many bullets so quickly, and this ammunition is cheap. Normal bullets are made of lead and are covered with copper. Both are incredibly soft and flexible metals. Unlike softer lead and copper bullets, steel bullets do not compress easily, and the steel of the bullet damages the steel of the gun barrel as it passes through. Steel bullets create a "shot out" barrel, ruining accuracy. It is like driving a car in the rain with no tread on the tires.

Much ammunition shot out of military assault-style weapons is steel bullets. I always run into people in the woods and tell them they are shooting steel bullets and ruining their firearms. The majority do not believe me. I carry a magnet and show them that their bullets are magnetic steel. They are destroying their guns with cheap ammunition and don't even know it.

Understanding ballistics and choosing the right caliber of weapon and the proper ammunition is necessary for gun ownership. This chapter will show photos of the parts of various bullets and cases used in modern firearms.

BULLET DETAILS

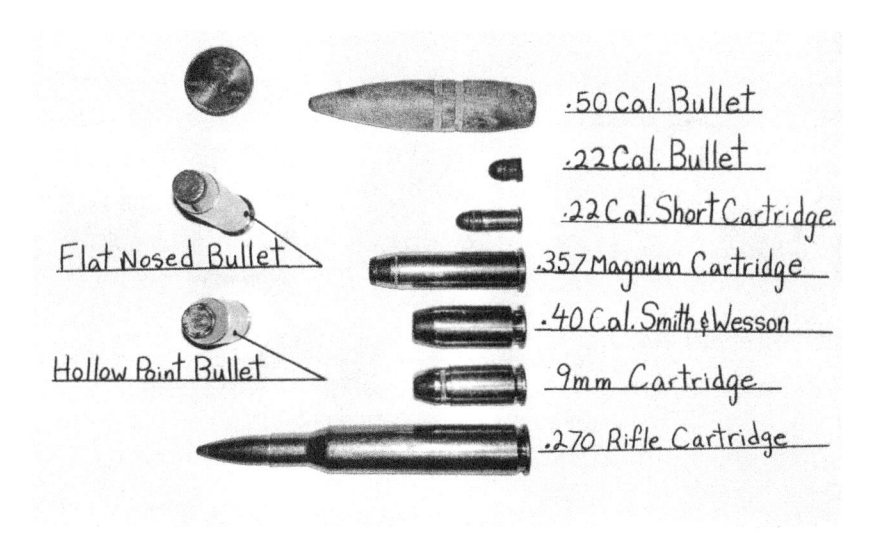

209

Typical bullets and cases - size comparison.

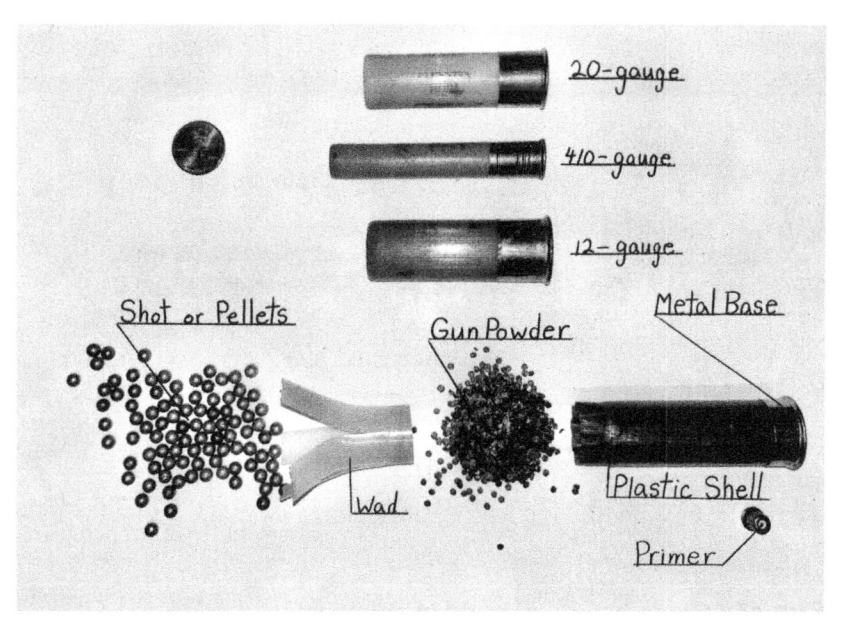

Inside a 12-guage shotgun round with BB-sized pellets, and three different size shotgun shells.

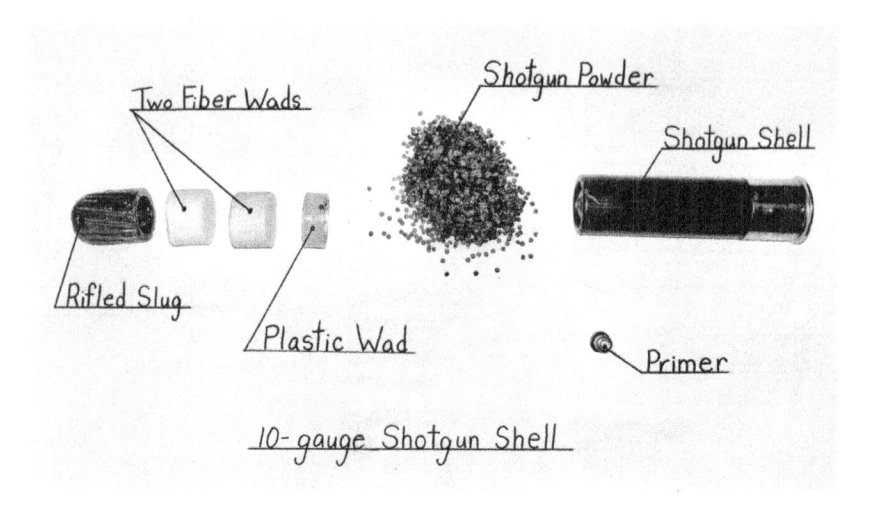

GUN GUIDE FOR DEMOCRATS

10-gauge Shotgun Shell (labels: Two Fiber Wads, Shotgun Powder, Shotgun Shell, Rifled Slug, Plastic Wad, Primer)

This 10-gauge shotgun round is the largest, and you can see the single large rifled slug that this one fires. It can shoot through a car or many walls.

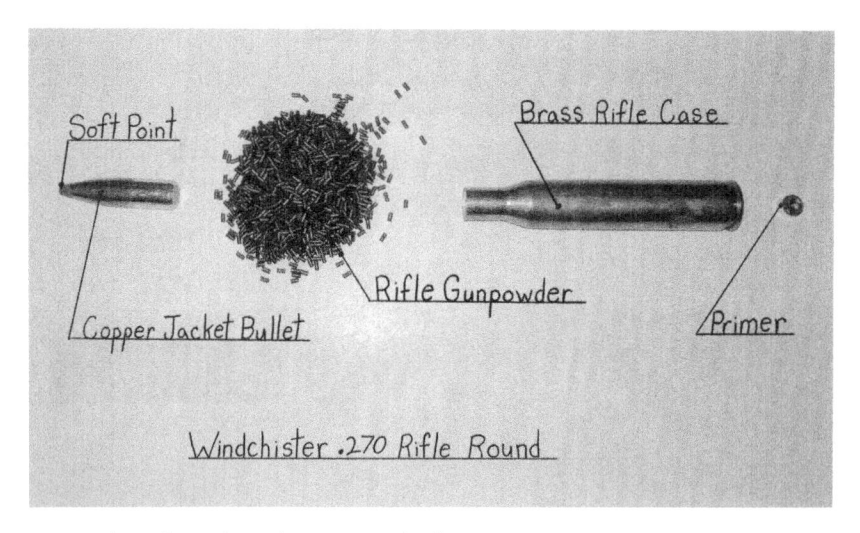

Windchister .270 Rifle Round (labels: Soft Point, Brass Rifle Case, Copper Jacket Bullet, Rifle Gunpowder, Primer)

Parts of a rifle or handgun round of ammunition.

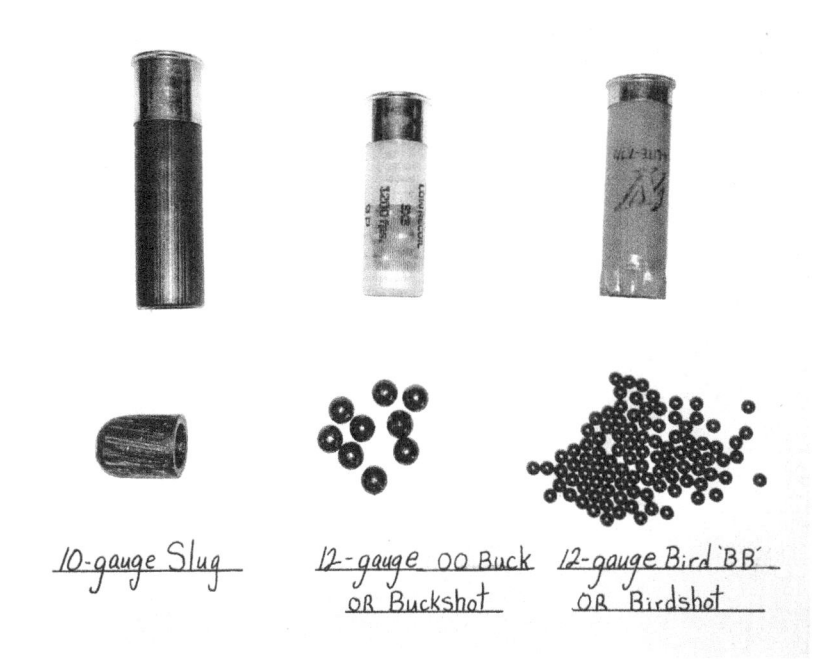

Comparison of shotgun projectiles sizes.

CLOSING NOTES

The first part of this book explains a lot about firearms, but more specifically, what shootings, tactical situations, and killing people is like. Very few books, instructors, or classes will approach firearms in such a way. They are all about learning the gun and how to hit a target, or even a person, but without information beyond that. They only cover about 1% of what you need to know if you want to be a safe and responsible gun owner. You are a fool if you buy a gun for self-protection and do not have this information first. If you can't kill a person and watch them die in front of you, in all the gory details, you should never own a firearm. It's that simple. Very few Americans have the necessary information before obtaining a firearm for self-defense. Those interested in buying a firearm in case a Trumpian or other right-wing nationalist dictatorship takes over America will find the necessary information in this book on how to do so safely. The book's first part is interesting, but the second part, although tedious, is also critical to safe firearm ownership and possession. I am not telling you to buy or not to buy a firearm; I am just telling you that you need to re-think what America teaches people about guns and go back to the basics and do it right if you plan to get one.

ACKNOWLEDGMENTS

I published my first book in August of 2021, called *Climbing Kilimanjaro With Africa's Top Guide by Erick Kivelege*. Erick was my partner on that project. That book is now available on Amazon around the world. In my first book project, I learned how many people are needed in a successful book project.

Like the Kili Book, this book also required the input of many people, from police work, the military, political leaders, educators, historians, and interested folks who shared their ideas, questions, opinions, and in some cases, their fears. It is customary to name and thank the people who spent hours being interviewed, helping with research, editing, or formatting a book, but this case is different. No one wanted to be named here in the acknowledgment section. They were all very supportive of the concept of this book and its being published, but they did not want to risk having their names printed here because they agreed with the book's lessons, such as "If you say something, say nothing." I understand, but thank them anonymously, all the same – they know who they are, and I appreciate all their hard work and encouragement. I would also say that this response to having their names in this section is one last warning about where our country is today. These are troubling times.

Also Available on Amazon today from Christopher Hurst:

Climbing Kilimanjaro With Africa's Top Guide by Erick Kivelege

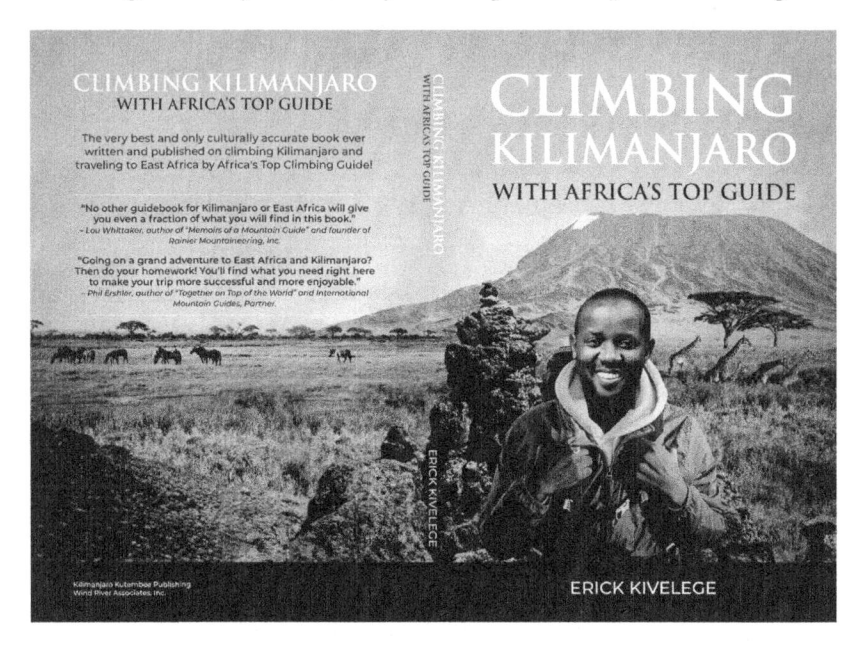

For decades, people traveling to East Africa have had to rely on guidebooks that have been written from a western or even a colonial point of view. Most of these books make mention of African savages being tamed by missionaries and lands being discovered and conquered by explorers. It's long past time for these old concepts to be put to rest and replaced with the true history of this remarkable land. This is the very best and only culturally accurate guidebook ever written and published on climbing Kilimanjaro and traveling to East Africa by Africa's Top Climbing Guide! No matter if you are a traveler, an armchair reader of exciting outdoor adventures, or just want to know the true story of East Africa, this book has it all. Here is a message from Erick on our book:

"For the very first time, here is the true story of Kilimanjaro and East Africa. As a Certified Climbing Guide, I have summited Kilimanjaro over 500 times. I was born and raised here in Moshi Town, Tanzania. I know this land, it's culture, and our people. This is a place of mystery and wonder like no other on earth. Past guidebooks by Westerners and Europeans can't give you even a fraction of what you will find in the pages of this book. They could never understand this land or Kilimanjaro as I do. Asante Sana (thank you!) for buying this book. I will welcome you on your journey of a lifetime to my homeland of East Africa and Kilimanjaro!"

You can buy it on Amazon today!

Made in the USA
Monee, IL
03 June 2023